SURVIVING
MIDDLE
SCHOOL

LUKE REYNOLDS

SURVIVING MIDDLE SCHOOL

Navigating the Halls,
Riding the Social Roller Coaster,
and Unmasking the Real You

ALADDIN
New York London Toronto Sydney New Delhi

BEYOND WORDS
Hillsboro, Oregon

ALADDIN
An imprint of Simon & Schuster
Children's Publishing Division
1230 Avenue of the Americas
New York, NY 10020

BEYOND WORDS
20827 N.W. Cornell Road, Suite 500
Hillsboro, Oregon 97124-9808
503-531-8700 / 503-531-8773 fax
www.beyondword.com

This Beyond Words/Aladdin edition July 2016
Text copyright © 2016 by Luke Reynolds
Illustrations copyright © 2016 by iStockphoto.com
Cover copyright © 2016 by Beyond Words/Simon & Schuster, Inc.
Cover illustrations copyright © 2016 by iStockphoto.com

For information about special discounts for bulk purchases, please contact Simon & Schuster
Special Sales at 1-866-506-1949 or business@simonandschuster.com.

The Simon & Schuster Speakers Bureau can bring authors to your live event. For more
information or to book an event contact the Simon & Schuster Speakers Bureau at
1-866-248-3049 or visit our website at www.simonspeakers.com.

Managing Editor: Lindsay S. Easterbrooks-Brown
Editors: Emmalisa Sparrow, Ali McCart, Nicole Geiger
Copyeditor: Henry Covey
Proofreader: Leah Brown
Interior and cover design: Sara E. Blum
Composition: William H. Brunson Typography Services
The text of this book was set in Bembo Std.

Manufactured in the United States of America 0122 SKY

10 9 8 7

Library of Congress Cataloging-in-Publication Data

Names: Reynolds, Luke, 1980– author.
Title: Surviving middle school : navigating the halls, riding the social roller coaster, and
    unmasking the real you / Luke Reynolds.
Description: New York : Aladdin ; Hillsboro, Oregon : Beyond Words, [2016] | Includes
    bibliographical references.
Identifiers: LCCN 2015040666 (print) | LCCN 2015051452 (ebook) |
    ISBN 9781582705545 (pbk.) | ISBN 9781582705552 (hardcover) |
    ISBN 9781481439213 (eBook)
Subjects: LCSH: Middle school students—Juvenile literature. | Middle school
    education—Juvenile literature. | Interpersonal relations—Juvenile literature. | Identity
    (Psychology)—Juvenile literature.
Classification: LCC LB1135 .R48 2016 (print) | LCC LB1135 (ebook) | DDC 373.18—dc23
LC record available at http://lccn.loc.gov/2015040666

To my four brothers—Christopher, Michael, Bryan, and Matthew—all weirdly wonderful and wonderfully weird

And to Mom and Dad, whom I won't call weird HERE, but . . . thanks for your support and for making so much pasta and garlic bread when I was growing up

CONTENTS

INTRODUCTION: DEFEATING THE SPACE GNOMES AND SAVING YOUR GARLIC BREAD

On my first day of seventh grade at Sage Park Middle School in Windsor, Connecticut, I walked through the front doors of the school, and time literally stopped. I mean—bam—clocks on the walls froze. Every single girl in the corridor looked at me with one thought bubble: *Wow, that guy is amazing.* And every middle school boy looked at me with the thought bubble: *Man, he is the total definition of awesome.* As I strolled through the hallways, I was so on fire that I singed the eyebrows of the principal *and* vice principal when they were welcoming all the new students. If you visit Sage Park, people still talk about it today.

On my first day of middle school, the following remarks could be overheard:

"Is that Brad Pitt?"

"My only wish this year is that *that* guy will date me / be my friend."

"I hope he'll autograph my notebook / say one word to me / look at me / acknowledge my existence / nod my way!"

"There goes absolute perfection."

A teacher was even believed to have said the following: "How am I going to teach that young man anything? His knowledge has to be as vast as the Mississippi River. He'll easily ace every assignment I have to give."

On my first day of middle school, I realized that I was the coolest thing since the school's last snow day.

On my first day of middle school, I was elected class president, chosen as captain of the basketball team, beat the school record in the 100-meter sprint, and wore attire straight out of an Abercrombie & Fitch catalog (who I was modeling for anyway, so I got the clothes for free).

On my first day of middle school, I was admitted to Harvard. After that, I was offered the lead role in a Hollywood movie. Then I received a call from the president of the United States asking for my thoughts on a decision he had to make. But I declined them all, because, hey, I wanted to focus on middle school.

On my first day of middle school . . .

Wait, my mother is now standing over my shoulder showing me the photograph of my eleven-year-old self on that very first day of middle school.

Wait, is that my hair sticking upward at the front like our toy poodle had licked it straight up?

Okay, sure, maybe my memory is a little foggy. Okay, maybe I've not actually recalled my own middle school experience because . . .

Wait, is that my face covered in an army of tiny black dots and tiny pus-filled white dots and tiny red dots that all were begging

for someone to connect all those dots so they could outline—yup—my face?

Wait, is that seriously a *Transformers* backpack I'm wearing?

Wait, am I really holding a *ThunderCats* metal lunchbox with Lion-O on the front? Seriously?

Wait, now my mom is telling me that when I came home after the first day of middle school, I was already crying because a very big eighth-grade boy (aka Goliath) had pushed me into a locker because I accidentally touched his elbow while I was trying to open my own locker, which wouldn't open because they gave me the wrong stupid combination?

Wait, now my older brothers are standing behind me, too, and they're reminding me that on my first day of middle school, my English teacher (Mrs. Macbeth) asked me to tell the class one thing I did over the past summer, and I responded by accidentally farting because I was so nervous? Seriously?

Wait, now my dad is standing behind me, next to my mom and my older brothers, and he is reminding me that on my *second* day of middle school, I told him that I quit middle school and that I quit life and that I quit being a stupid, nervous, fart-responding, zit-covered, Goliath-punching-bag kid?

Hmmm. Weird. That's not how I remember it.

If you're anything like me when I was in middle school, maybe you crave the first kind of experience: You want it to be perfect. You want to be popular. You want to look right. You don't want to be made fun of, or pushed around, or ignored, or be given the wrong stupid locker combination.

The bad news is that everything I just wrote in that first experience is impossible. Because you are human, and because you are in middle school, you're going to hit some bumps. Some will be little bumps, the kind you could take on a sled while cruising down the hill in your neighborhood and turn into awesome jumps. Others are going to be big bumps, the kind you slam into on your sled and knock you flat on the ground and leave you bleeding, freezing, and thinking: *This absolutely sucks.* And to top it off, you want to cry, but you don't cry because—hey—you're in middle school.

So the perfect middle school experience doesn't exist.

And there will be bumps.

But even though the truth about middle school is that it's bumpy in all kinds of ways, the other important truth is that you can get through those bumps without giving up who you really are. You can get over those bumps without being terrified of not being popular, or having the right logo on your clothes, or saying and doing the "wrong" thing. You can get through middle school without losing that inner voice that makes you unique, passionate, funny, kind, strong, and bold.

You can make it through middle school and be who you really are.

After going through my fair share of bumps as a student, I decided to go back to middle school. Not because I didn't pass the first time around—and not because I wanted to answer Mrs. Macbeth's question without farting or to face off against Goliath (both of whom, I hear, are still at Sage Park). Instead, I went back to middle school to be an English teacher. And I learned some things that I think you'll want to know. They're good. Some of them are juicy. Juicier than an orange being squeezed by Goliath. You'll like these things I learned. (I promise.)

Have you ever walked past a playground where you used to go as a little kid and looked at the slide and thought, *I used to be afraid of that puny little thing?* Even though a lot of things terrified me during my own middle school years, when I returned as a teacher, it was like someone gave me binoculars. Or a telescope. Or a microscope. Or a surround sound speaker system. (You pick the device.) And what had seemed so blurry and muffled before became as clear as a crisp clap in a silent hallway. As a middle school student, you may be lost in your own vision of how screwed up and weird you think you are, but here's the thing: You're not screwed up, I promise. But you are weird. And so am I. And so is everybody. Be weird!

I am weird, you are weird. Everyone in this world is weird.

—Theodor Geisel (Dr. Seuss), insanely brilliant (and weird) author and artist who loved cats in hats

So as long as we're in agreement that you're weird, I'm weird, and *everyone is weird*, let's be weird together, okay? Cool. So if we agree that you and I are going to be weird together, we might as well not waste any time with a normal, boring book. Therefore, this book is weird. *Very* weird.

But it will help you survive middle school and be yourself. There are going to be a lot of forces fighting against you: bullies, grades, comparisons, competitions, insecurity, and fear, not to mention things like advertisements, wearing the "right" clothes, listening to the right music, and having the right body type and ideas. All of these things that fight you are like an army of space gnomes who are after only one thing: garlic bread.

Yes. Space gnomes crave garlic bread and will stop at nothing until they get it. And the cool (and kind of scary) thing is this: you've got loads.

Buttery goodness!

Garlicky taste!

Warm, freshly baked bread!

All melted and squishing together!

The battle lines are drawn. It's you against the space gnomes. You've got the power to make your middle school experience different from mine. You can defeat the space gnomes and protect your garlic bread. You can make it through middle school being the real you.

Here's how.

1

COMPARING IS FOR MELTED BUTTER ONLY

ere's where you see what a secret agent of the space gnomes, the colors purple and pink, President Teddy Roosevelt, and talking to yourself (out loud) all have in common. Hint: the answer is *not* that you can dip them all in chocolate sauce and then put them on your ice cream as a topping.

A STORY ABOUT A SHIRT

One of my seventh-grade students arrived early to class one day. Let's call him Perspicacious so that we can hide his real name (which was Henry). Perspicacious wanted more than anything to be popular. Perspicacious tried to make sure he wore the right clothes with all the right brand names on them; he tried to laugh at the right times; he tried to get his biceps to be just the right size. So this one day, Perspicacious walked into my classroom wearing a purple shirt. I thought it looked awesome. It had buttons right down the front, a collar so sharp you could slice a finger on it, and the sleeves rolled up like he was ready to build a house.

> Perspicacious: Do you like my new shirt, Mr. Reynolds?

> Me: Yeah, it's awesome, man. I need to get one too, because I bet my wife, Jennifer, will love me in a shirt that looks as good as that one.

Perspicacious smiled and then started to open up his backpack and pull out some books and his binder. The sun was shining in full force even though it was winter in New England. Soon, other students began to trickle into the classroom. One of the first guys in the door (we'll call him Foggy Foggerson), brought his hand up to cover his mouth and started laughing as he pointed at Perspicacious's purple shirt.

Foggy Foggerson: Man, are you pretending to be Barney or something? Are you a purple dinosaur?

Perspicacious's just-beaming face grew red and shot downward like he was inspecting the floor for ants. Foggy Foggerson continued to laugh, and as other students walked into the classroom, they followed Foggy Foggerson's example and laughed at Perspicacious's purple shirt. I stood up from my desk and asked Foggy Foggerson to come out into the hallway with me. The laughter died down immediately. Foggy Foggerson got an earful in the hall from me, but the silence that ensued inside the classroom was crushing Perspicacious. When I came back into the classroom with Foggy Foggerson in tow, Perspicacious asked me if he could use the bathroom. He came back wearing a white T-shirt—his undershirt—instead of the purple shirt he'd thought was so dang suave only a few minutes before.

So what happened? The purple shirt didn't suddenly, all by itself, become something Perspicacious hated. Foggy Foggerson used the potent words of comparison to convince Perspicacious that his wardrobe was severely lacking. Ugly. Laughable.

Comparing can help us in some ways—say, for instance, when we are comparing how much butter is on one slice of garlic bread versus another, and we need to consider how buttery we're feeling. But in middle school, comparison means thinking about how you measure up against someone else. And often, it sure feels like you don't. Something you absolutely love and swear by is fodder for someone else to laugh at and totally mock. The music you listen to, the way you wear your hair, the grades you get, the people you're friends with, the movies you like—heck, even the color of your eyes. Everything is up for comparison, and if you don't learn to let yourself love what you actually love (instead of what everyone else tells you to love), comparison is going to rob you of everything you enjoy and so much of who you are, the way it did to Perspicacious that morning.

Every student I have ever taught in middle school has always carried around in his or her head a little voice that whispered things like: *You're not as good as her. You're not as tough as him. You didn't get grades as high as she did. You're not as hot as he is. You're not as funny as she is. You're not as popular as he is. Your clothes don't look as cool or cute or tough or sexy as his or hers or theirs . . .*

So what can be done? How could Perspicacious find the same joy in his purple shirt that he'd had when he first entered class that morning, before comparison (which was speaking through Foggy Foggerson) stole that joy away?

A DEAD PRESIDENT SPEAKS TO STOP THE SPACE GNOMES

A very close friend of mine once shared with me the *big* secret of how comparison works. Once we know the secret of how something works, it's a lot easier to beat it. Consider your favorite video game, a softball match, a swimming competition, an upcoming test, or any other challenge you face: as soon as you know how the game *really* works, everything makes a lot more sense. Once you get the rules and see how to practice, you can make it to the next level or win the game or ace the test. The problem is that most of us don't ever learn the real truth about comparison. Instead, we keep thinking that comparison is good, that it's somehow right to see how we measure up against everyone else—from test scores to styles to biceps to breasts. It's not.

So if comparison is definitely not good, then what exactly is it? And how do we know for sure? The real scoop about comparison is that it is actually an elite secret agent of the space gnomes. Its job? Yup: stealing. Comparison is out for one thing and one thing alone: to steal joy. Imagine this: You are sitting at your dinner table when out comes a whole plate of warm, buttery goodness in the shape of garlic bread. It is soft. It is squishy. It positively makes your mouth salivate and your skin get goose bumps while your tongue falls out of your mouth and you actually start *panting* and—

Bam! An elite agent of the space gnomes busts into your dining room and swipes the garlic bread. The whole loaf.

Gone!

Ahhhh!

And who was that elite space-gnomey secret agent? That agent was Comparison, who is nothing more than a garlic bread bandit, a thief of your *almost*-joy.

But don't just take my word for it. I've got an actual quote to prove it to you. Shrouded in mystery—no one knows for sure who said it—this single line tells us the truth about who Comparison really is. And even though no one really knows who first said the line, some people think a dead president said it (before he died, of course). And I happen to agree.

So here's the real scoop about Comparison. Are you ready?

Are you sure?

Then let's scoop it up. President Teddy Roosevelt (we think, but aren't certain) said: "Comparison is the thief of joy."

My brother-in-law, Paul, shared those powerful words with me a long time ago, back before cell phones could take pictures. (By the way, that thieving Comparison absolutely loves to steal your joy by having you look at other kids' cell phone pictures. Comparison robs by saying: *You need to look/act/think more like her and him and this clip and that image and everything except who you really are!*)

In middle school, you're going to find (or you've already found, if you're a student now) that a thousand times a day, a small voice inside your head is going to ask you to compare yourself with everyone else around you. And even if you're able to quiet down that voice a little—say, when you're laughing and having fun and relaxed and learning and excited—then it often seems like another student (or sometimes even a teacher) is right there ready to compare you to something or someone else and tell you why you're not measuring up.

Comparison is the thief of joy.
—Attributed to Theodore Roosevelt,
26th President of the United States (and who was a big softie)

The problem with giving in to that voice is that it only makes you feel a whole lot crappier. The other problem is that you can never see what's inside another student's head or heart. So while on the outside some people look like they've got it all—good looks, a sense of humor, high grades, popularity, the right kinds of clothes—what you don't know is that there's a likely chance these people are crying themselves to sleep every night. Why? Because even they feel like they're not good enough in comparison with other people.

As a student, I often walked around the hallways of my middle school just seeing things in other people that made me look bad. And at night, I would go home and try to change myself so I could be cooler, or more popular, or better looking, or anything else. But it never worked, because I was always trying to change from something that I was into something that I *wasn't*. I was trying to force myself to like different things, think different things, and become different things. And that's an endlessly losing battle.

So what's the real battle—and how do you even try to win it in middle school? The real battle is learning to protect the real you from the shoplifting work of Comparison—not in finding the "right" stuff to think, do, believe, and wear. And you start fighting the real battle when you truly believe this line: "Comparison is the thief of joy."

Say you get an essay back, and you receive a B on it, and you've worked your butt off (and have found a way to reattach your butt after working it off), and you did your best. Then a B is a gold medal on this essay for you, the best possible cheesecake at the best possible restaurant on the best possible plate served by the best possible server. Bs are awesome. Getting a B rocks. Smile to yourself and reach around to pat yourself on the back (after making sure your butt has successfully been reattached after all that work).

But if your friend then gets his or her essay back, and there's a big bloated A on that piece of paper—and that piece of paper is most definitely not your essay—beware, because Comparison is getting ready to swoop in and steal that joy from you. Comparison says, *Proud of your B? Really? It's nothing like that A! I mean, come on, that A is basically a rocket blasting off to the moon! It's shaped that way. See its point there? Blasting toward the moon with that point leading the way! Does your B happen to have a point? No? Just a bunch of curves and a straight line? Oh. You'll never see the stars that way! All you'll see are those obnoxious space gnomes flying around with their jet packs and threatening to rob you. So there. And that means your friend's essay was awesome while yours was just okay. I guess you're an okay student. Nothing great. Nothing worthy of the moon or stars.*

Or say you run the mile during gym class, and you do it in nine minutes flat, and you worked your butt off (but, yes, of course, you reattach it afterward), then nine minutes is freaking awesome. Gold medal. Marvelous. But maybe your friend—you notice—did it in seven minutes flat, and the space gnomes' elite secret agent, Comparison, swoops in again. He says, *Whoa! That's two whole minutes faster than you. Your nine minutes is awful! What? I don't care that you can barely breathe; you're nothing compared to your gifted runner friend. And did you even happen to notice that the gym teacher was talking to your friend about going out for track? Did you notice that the gym teacher NEVER mentioned track to you? And did you also notice how everyone else was watching your friend and definitely NOT watching you?*

Or say you come into class one morning wearing a purple shirt that you think is pretty cool, and you feel good in it, and you're smiling, then you're being yourself. You chose that shirt at the store, brought it home, put it on this morning. You didn't choose it because the label was the "right" label. You didn't pick it because you saw everyone else wearing it and then begged, pleaded, and threatened your mom or dad until they forked over a hundred bucks for you to get it too. No. You just liked it. It felt natural for you to put it on. But then someone named Foggy Foggerson didn't think so. And he compared you to a big purple dinosaur, and it made you realize that your *stupid, stupid, stupid* purple shirt is *definitely* NOT in style. So you go to the bathroom, cry a little, and take the *stupid, stupid, stupid* shirt off.

In all of these cases, remember that the real battle is not about a grade or running or clothes. No. The real battle is all about comparison and the theft of who you really are. By giving in to that dangerous voice—the voice telling you that you're not as good as, not as fast as, not as fashionable as—you allow comparison to steal the real you. And you are too important, too essential to this world, too irreplaceable to allow a measly agent of the space gnomes to steal your contribution to life.

WHAT ABOUT PERSPICACIOUS?

When Perspicacious came back into my classroom that day wearing his white T-shirt, I knew something inside him had broken. Foggy Foggerson was employing that stealthy thief, Comparison—*Bam, baby! Your shirt is hideous, not as cool as anything my friends or I wear!*—and Perspicacious had no protection. At the end of the school day,

I asked Perspicacious to stay after with me, and I told him about that line: "Comparison is the thief of joy." He nodded glumly. We moved on to work on some homework, and then he got on the late bus and went home.

The next day, Perspicacious was wearing a name-brand, normal, fit-in shirt. But he asked if he could stay after school. And we talked some more about that line: "Comparison is the thief of joy." I told Perspicacious what you've already heard—that I went through my own middle school years constantly changing from something I was into something I *wasn't*. Perspicacious nodded glumly. And then we repeated yesterday's pattern: homework, followed by the late bus.

To be yourself in a world that is constantly trying to make you something else is the greatest accomplishment.
—Ralph Waldo Emerson, writer from the 1800's who hugged *a lot* of trees

Day after day, Perspicacious stayed after school, and we talked about that single line—*one line!*—over and over and over again. Until finally, about a month later, Perspicacious walked into class one day. And he was wearing . . .

A pink shirt. It had buttons right down the front, a collar so sharp you could slice a finger on it, and the sleeves rolled up like he was ready to build a house.

And the *next* day, he wore his purple shirt.

For about a week, he went back and forth: pink shirt, purple shirt, pink shirt, purple shirt, pink shirt.

Now, I wish I could lie a little here and tell you that on the first day that Perspicacious proudly wore his pink shirt, everyone else in the middle school stood and applauded his bravery (because that's what bravery *is*). They didn't. Foggy Foggerson still laughed. Other students still made fun of him. But when Perspicacious wore his purple shirt the day after, Foggy Foggerson was a little quieter. So were the other students. And on the third day, when Perspicacious went back to his pink shirt, a girl in the class even told Perspicacious that she thought he looked pretty "hot."

By the end of the week, Perspicacious wore his pink shirt with a massive smile across his face. And because he wore it with such pride and fearlessness and *bravery*, it kind of made other people stop sending Comparison after his joy. They gave up. They saw Perspicacious wasn't going to change, so they stopped trying to get him to change.

WHAT ABOUT YOU?

Here's what you have to do: Stop listening to the voice of Comparison. Stop letting the space gnomes steal all your garlic bread, because they *will eat all that buttery, garlicky goodness if you just sit there and let them.*

Stop. And I don't mean stop as in the way your mom or dad rolls through a stop sign, pretending to hit the brakes.

I mean, STOP!!!!

The more you pay attention to that voice of Comparison in your head, the crappier you're going to feel about who you are. Because the thing is, there are always going to be people around you who *look* like they can do whatever you can do, but better. And they are always going to be very sure to tell you they think they do it (dress, think, act, play sports) better. You are going to drive yourself crazy in middle school if you compare your grades, your looks, your popularity, your friends, your boyfriend or girlfriend, the color of your shirt, or anything else with others.

"Comparison is the thief of joy."

Instead of comparing, and caving in to that voice, you can start by thinking about what you enjoy, what you do well, and what makes your heart skip a beat. What makes you feel really excited and alive and happy? For each of us, it's something different that gets our heart beating fast. It's big things and little things. For Perspicacious, it started with a purple shirt. He loved it, and it felt good on him. What is it for you? What are the things that you naturally like— things you enjoy doing, ways you enjoy talking, clothes you enjoy wearing?

**Don't ask what the world needs.
Ask what makes you come alive, and go do it.
Because what the world needs is
people who have come alive.**
—Howard Thurman, author and civil rights leader who wore boldness like armor

EXERCISE
Your Security System:
Make a List but DON'T Check It Twice

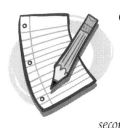

Grab a piece of paper (or use your journal if you keep one, or a doc on your computer, or any writing-capable gadget you possess!) and make a list of everything you enjoy that comes to your mind. *Don't second-guess yourself.* Just as soon as something pops into your head, write it down. It could be clothes, activities, things you find funny, movies you like, colors you're drawn to, books you love, and so on. And if you don't want to write, doodle. And if you don't want to doodle, create a secret code that only you know and create a whole new alphabet that records that secret code, and then use that secret code to record things on your list. (However, it may be a whole lot easier to just choose the writing or doodling option.) On your paper (or whatever you're using to journal) you can call your list:

My List of Stuff I Enjoy

All right. Good. You've now got a whole list of things that *you* enjoy, not because other people in middle school told you that you *should* enjoy them but simply because they bring delight to you—they are the styles, ideas, things, and activities you love doing simply because they're a part of what make you yourself.

But let's go for one more list. Let's be crazy. Let's pretend we're on a mission to catch those space gnomes and take back our joy! But the only way to find our way back to Planet Earth is for us to make one more list—right now—about who we really are. The stuff we know to be true about who we are.

On this list, write down (or doodle, or, yup, make a secret code of) everything you know to be true about yourself and everything you really love about yourself—whether big or small or important or not. Not stuff you want to try to become, not things you want to change, but what's true about you right now and what you want to appreciate about the super-awesome you. For instance, if you love laughing—*bam!*—"I love laughing" goes on the list. If you know you are a kind person—*bam!*—"I am kind to others" goes on the list.

Ready? No second-guessing. No telling yourself that a certain quality or characteristic isn't worthy of recording here. (By the way, on my own list, I've recorded the fact that I know I am weird, including my obsession with space gnomes.) Okay, go.

Things I Know to Be True about Myself— and Why I Rock

Great stuff. These two lists are now evidence for you. Every time you go to middle school and come home feeling like that thief Comparison has been robbing you, look at these lists. Remember what you love. Remember who you are. And trust *that* person instead of Comparison. After all, you've lived with yourself for a whole bunch of years by now. Comparison hasn't had you on his radar all that long. Who knows you better? You or Comparison? And no matter how stealthy Comparison is, you can be like Perspicacious. You can choose—again and again and again—to wear what *you* like, to act naturally, to love what *you* love, and to keep choosing it.

Comparison is a hard thief to stop, but it can be stopped. It takes practice. It takes work. (But remember, you're used to working your butt off and then reattaching it again.) In the beginning, you may even have to say out loud to yourself (either alone or in public, the latter if you don't care about people asking, "Did you know that person has imaginary friends?"): "I am not going to let you rob me, Comparison! I am not going to compare myself to others! No, I am not going to let you and your space gnome commanders steal all my garlic bread!"

You may have to tell yourself things like that *a lot*. (Out loud.) You may have to read and re-read your lists *a lot*. (Out loud.) Hey, I still need to say that to myself and re-read my lists. And you may have to write the line **COMPARISON IS THE THIEF OF JOY** in big, bold letters and put it somewhere you'll see it often.

But the good news is, the more you start to realize when that little thief Comparison is attacking you, the more you'll be able to stop this and replace it with thoughts that actually help you. And the more you stop that thief, the more joy you'll feel inside.

You can fight Comparison. And you can win. I believe in you. You're stronger than it is. I know because I watch my own students fight it, and when they beat it, beautiful things begin to happen in their lives and inside their hearts.

And if you desperately feel the need to compare something, the next time you're sitting down to a meal of pasta loaded with saucy sauce, glance over toward that fresh, buttery garlic bread and compare the melted butter across the loaf: Where are the deepest pockets of buttery goodness? In what order should you eat them? That's about the only comparison worth your time and energy in middle school.

2

BE LIKE
CAKED DIRT

Here's where you see what bike tires, Thomas Edison, glossy magazines, and failure all have in common. Hint: it's *not* that you can paint all of these things blue and then juggle them.

A STORY ABOUT SOME BIKE TIRES

When I was in middle school, I loved riding my bike. I would ride it all over my neighborhood, all over my friends' neighborhoods, and all over the neighborhoods of people I didn't know. I rode my bike to the little convenience store at a nearby gas station (where I'd buy as much candy as I could for the few dollars I had managed to get from my mom). If there was a place I could ride a bike, I rode mine there.

But there was one thing I absolutely hated about taking my bike so many places: the dirt. If it was even a little wet out (which it often was), my wheels would get totally covered with thickish mud. This mud would joyfully shoot off my tires and straight onto . . . you guessed it, the butt crack area of my pants. And, as you well know, the last thing you need in middle school is pants that have dirt stains all along the butt crack area.

As if having dark mud stains on the back of my pants wasn't bad enough, there was the added horror of the eventual caked-on dirt on my wheels after riding in the rain. Once my bike was tucked into our warm garage, all that mud would rapidly turn into caked-on dirt, and if I didn't chip away at it after each day of wet riding, it would verifiably become cemented to my wheels. The thing about cemented caked dirt is that it doesn't like to say good-bye to whatever it's holding on to. It hangs in there, relentlessly, no matter how hard you chip away at it. Sure, pieces of it may fall off, but mostly it just digs its teeth in and says, "Heck no, I'm not going anywhere!" And then, eventually, the caked dirt would cement and turn steel-like.

Even though caked dirt on a bike is an awful, downright treacherous thing, here's the awesome news: somewhere inside you, there is a big quarry of caked dirt, a whole mound of it, and the thing about *this* particular kind of caked dirt inside you is that even the space gnomes aren't going to be able to break it apart. (However, as you know by now, the space gnomes will do whatever it takes to steal your garlic bread—and if it takes chipping away at your caked dirt to crack it, they will!) You might not actually have known up until now that this caked dirt is inside you, waiting to be found. But it is there, I promise!

The caked dirt inside you can see how hard the test / homework / essay / lab experiment / speech / presentation is, and yet help you to work your butt off to do it anyway. When you feel like flopping down directly on your face and saying, "Ahhhhhh! I can't do this!" you keep going anyway because, hey, you've got caked dirt inside of you.

This caked dirt you've got is the part of you that feels how hard life is for your family, for your friends, for characters you read about in books, and for real people you read about in newspapers and see in documentaries, but you keep going anyway. And you try to help others to keep going anyway too—because, yup, you've got caked dirt inside of you. (And other people have got caked dirt inside of *them* too.)

And no matter what kinds of tools those stealthy space gnomes wield to try to chip away at your caked dirt (Chisels! Screwdrivers!

Chainsaws! Knives capable of cutting through quarters!), as long as you *keep going*, there is no way they can cut or chop apart your caked dirt and steal it away from you.

And the way to keep going is to do on the outside what the caked dirt does on the inside.

> Children, if you are tired, keep going; if you are scared, keep going; if you are hungry, keep going; if you want to taste freedom, keep going.
>
> —Attributed to Harriet Tubman, who escaped slavery and then repeatedly led many others to freedom

---

EXERCISE
Time to Fail!

Before we get any further, take three minutes and write down something that you tried or wanted to accomplish but failed at. It could be something huge or something tiny. It could be that you wanted to score a goal at your next soccer game, or that you wanted to get an A on your school assignment, or that you wanted to try talking to your dad or mom about that thing that was bothering you a whole heck of a lot, or that you wanted to try to learn to play the flute, or that you wanted to make it to the peak of a towering mountain. Whatever story comes to mind, just take those three minutes and write the experience of your failure on a piece of paper or in your journal.

Ready? Here's your title:

My Three-Minute Story of Failure

Write that title at the top of your story. Fabulous. Now, keep this three-minute story of failure nearby, and we'll get back to it toward the end of the chapter. But first, I want to tell you about writing and a student named Planetarium.

AGAIN, AND AGAIN, AND AGAIN, AND . . .

When I became a middle school English teacher, there was one thing I was absolutely certain about: I knew I wanted to give my students long, difficult writing assignments. Not because I wanted to be a jerk, but because I knew that if I could help my students become good writers—and hard workers—I would be giving them a great gift in the world. No matter what you're going to do with your life, you're going to need to write well. (Even engineers have to write good emails, letters, and descriptions of their projects.) But whenever I assigned an essay, I found that students often just glanced at their scores as I returned their papers, shoved the essays in their backpacks, and that was the end of that. Most of my students never looked at their essays again.

So I devised a scheme to get my students (well, most of them) to look at the essays again, and again, and again. One day in class, just before handing back their latest essay assignment, I told my students that the grades they saw on their essays were not final. I told them that they could keep working on their essays as much as they wanted, and their grade would keep going up with the new work that they did on their essays.

One of my students responded, "So, like, you mean we can all get 100s on our essays?"

"Yes," I replied.

That same student said, "You mean, like, we can just keep rewriting our essays again and again and make lots of changes and improvements and revisions until you tell us they're as good as they can be?"

"Yes," I replied.

"No stinking way!" my student exclaimed.

"Yes stinking way," I replied.

What my students thought was just incredibly nice of me was actually the definition of what writing is: you write, and write, and write, then you revise, and edit, and revise, and edit, and go on and on and on until it's as good as it can be. After all, even Ernest Hemingway revised many parts of his novels more than twenty or thirty times before he felt they were finished. (Once, he rewrote the ending to one of his novels *thirty-nine times.*[1] Talk about some serious inner caked dirt!)

**It's not that I'm so smart.
It's just that I stay with problems longer.**
—Albert Einstein, brilliant mathematician who got low grades
and boycotted hair-combing

I stressed to my students that it wasn't about getting a perfect score—even though many of them were excited by that prospect—it was about teaching them to produce the best possible writing they could.

And so we set off as a class on this new way of writing and grading, where every student had a different due date depending on which draft of an essay they were on.

PLANETARIUM ~~STRIKES~~ WRITES AGAIN!

Why do I tell you all of this when we were having a super-cool discussion about caked dirt? Good question. One of my students—I'll call her Planetarium—decided to really take me up on my offer. So for every essay she wrote for English that year, she revised any areas that weren't as strong as they could be. She didn't really seem to care about the grade. She loved writing, and she told me she wanted her writing to be the very best it could be. (Notice, she didn't want her writing to be *better than* anyone else's, and she didn't just want to get a bunch of As on her papers. She wanted to become the best writer she could become.)

For one essay, she completed eleven drafts. I'm not kidding. She kept writing, and revising, and writing, and editing, and writing, and revising, and writing, and editing, and revising, and editing, and writing.

Planetarium did indeed become an incredible writer by the end of the year. She was like caked dirt. No matter what, she refused to give up, or give in, or accept anything less than her very best. Sometimes, I know I drove Planetarium a bit crazy. After all, by the ninth and tenth drafts, we were focusing on things like mood and tone and allusion and extended metaphor and parallelism. But she kept telling me that she wanted to do whatever it took to make her writing as strong as it could become.

Planetarium was like caked dirt, and that's exactly how you need to be. Friends may tell you to give up. Parents may sometimes tell you to give up. Heck, some teachers may tell you to give up. But maybe they're not seeing what's really inside of you—maybe they're not seeing the person you can become, the person you *want* to become.

LIGHTS, CAMERA, LIES

In middle school, it's going to sound really good to give up on something if it doesn't come easily. Think of the glossy magazine covers you see in every grocery store checkout aisle and the posters plastered all over the mall. These magazine covers scream at you how to be "perfect" at all kinds of things—and how to do it quickly.

First, the stuff they're trying to get you to be perfect at—*Destroy all acne! Grow biceps the size of Texas plus California! Grow breasts the size of Texas plus California plus Arkansas! Be as tough as a tiger genetically combined with a lion and a rhino!*—is actually physically impossible to achieve (we'll talk more about this in chapter 3).

But the second thing these magazine covers and posters do is they tell us that everything should be easy. Getting in shape, making great friends, doing well in school, learning to play a sport, learning an instrument, protecting our garlic bread from being stolen by the space gnomes—none of this stuff is easy. It's hard work, during which we all have to learn to be like caked dirt. The magazine covers and posters suggest it's easy, but they're selling us all a big lie (and making some great money doing so).

Movies do this to us too. In a movie, we see somebody try for something: make the basketball team, find a best friend, save the universe, eat fifty pizzas in a single meal. Whatever battle the protagonist in the movie is trying to win, she or he has to work hard to do it, and may fail a bit, but then—eventually—victory, yes! But when we watch this, we see it all happen *in about two hours*. In real life—*in middle school*—the victory can sometimes take two months, two years, or even longer! Learning to play basketball or the guitar, writing a great essay, finding a true friend—these things take work, and they don't happen in the montage of a few scenes.

WAS THOMAS EDISON LIKE CAKED DIRT? YES!

If you love something or if you know something is true about yourself, and you fail, or flop, or just plain *really, really want to STOP*, then it's time to close your eyes and imagine that you are caked dirt— that just because you got chipped away at a little because you failed once, or you didn't make the team, or you didn't get the grade you wanted, or that friendship didn't turn out the way you'd hoped, it's not over. The movie of your life is a heck of a lot longer than two hours.

The famous inventor Thomas Edison (who invented the lightbulb and—hey!—was one of the inventors of the movie camera) once said in reply to criticism for some of his failed inventions, "I have not failed. I've just found 10,000 ways that won't work." Edison was like caked dirt. He knew that the times he failed and didn't do what he really wanted to do were teaching him about the inventions he would create later. He knew that the only way to become who you really are is by holding on through lots of pain and struggle and failure.

> **It's only those who do nothing that make no mistakes.**
>
> —Joseph Conrad, Polish novelist from the turn of the twentieth-century who believed in truth, no matter how hard it was to find

Whenever you feel like giving up on something good and meaningful and true in your life, think of caked dirt. Then, hang in there just a little bit longer. If you do, you'll find that there isn't any weapon the world can wield to knock you down for good.

Now, before we say good-bye in this chapter, I want you to do one thing. Go back to that three-minute story of your failure. Where the word *Failure* appears in the heading, cross it out and write *Inventing*.

Why? Because failure is a chance to invent another possibility. If you can see your moment of terrible failure this way, then you've actually had a pretty cool success. The failure still hurts—I know—but it's not final. (Remember, you've got caked dirt inside you and you're not giving up!) So failure is not the last word. And our mushy, gushy brains start to actually see our experience of falling flat on our face as one more step toward who we really are rather than as a total waste of time.

Plus, seeing our failure as inventing kind of shocks the space gnomes. While they're eyeballing us and mocking us for our failures—*bam!*— we get back up and kick the ball again, rewrite the essay again, talk to that friend again. This kind of thing makes the space gnomes both furious and more than a little powerless. The garlic bread they're trying to steal slips from their gnomey hands and into ours.

> **Keep away from people who try to belittle your ambitions. Small people always do that, but the really great make you feel that you, too, can become great.**
> —Mark Twain, author from the 1800's who had a bushy white mustache and was a part-time stand-up comedian

So fail.

Yes!

I still fail. All of my friends still fail. Even people who are about three times my age still fail. *Everybody fails.* But we can choose to be like caked dirt, which hangs on so long it basically turns to steel, or we can let go and tumble off the tires to the ground where we'll get stepped on. By seeing your failures as inventing moments, I promise you're going to have one heck of a better ride.

3

WHAT DO I THINK ABOUT THAT? LET ME THINK ABOUT THAT...

Here's where you see what your billions of gooey brain cells, Mr. Buttmuncher, hot girls and guys, and recycled clothing have in common. Hint: it's *not* that they have all landed on the moon.

A STORY ABOUT A COOL KID

One year, on the first day of school, a seventh-grade girl walked into my homeroom with two other girls in tow. On her way to a group of desks in the back row, she passed a girl and said, "Still got your hairstyle from third grade, I see." The sting hit its mark, and the girl who'd been ridiculed shrunk in her seat.

Various students in the room laughed.

The mean girl—we'll call her Philharmonic—continued to move around the room, eyeballing other students and making snide comments. Her two friends followed closely behind and chattered together while she commented.

I quickly asked Philharmonic to have a chat with me in the hallway. She huffed and puffed but finally followed. Once out in the hall, she agreed she'd been unkind and promised she would no longer make those remarks.

But every homeroom after that, she entered the classroom with earphones on and hooked up to her music player. Every day, Philharmonic refused to talk to any other students and just listened to her music. Her two friends eventually brought in their own earphones and did the same. When I finally asked Philharmonic what her music of choice was, she scoffed and replied, "Only the top hits. What else?" Then rolled her eyes.

The next day, in homeroom, the students entered to the booming sounds of the a cappella group Ladysmith Black Mambazo (one of my favorite music groups), who I was blasting from my CD player. Philharmonic tried desperately to listen to her own music, but Ladysmith Black Mambazo drowned out her playlist of top hits. Day after day, my music blared, and day after day, Philharmonic grew angrier and angrier.

Then another girl started singing along. And then a boy. And then another boy. And then another girl. Soon, the homeroom had a favorite Ladysmith Black Mambazo song, and every morning they requested it. (It's an amazing song, by the way, if you're interested—called "Homeless.") And then, one day, one of Philharmonic's friends—a so-called "cool kid," who I'll call Shooting Star—started singing along with the song too.

I wish I could tell you that Philharmonic came in the next day and started whooping it up for Ladysmith (huzzah!), but she didn't. However, the so-called cool kid—Shooting Star—*did*. She had decided one normal homeroom morning to start thinking for herself—no matter what the leader of her group chose. An incredibly wise man who lived alone in the woods for a while, Henry David Thoreau, would have loved what Shooting Star did. To paraphrase one of his most important ideas: If a seventh grade girl does not keep pace with her companions, perhaps it is because she hears the beat of a different drummer. Let her step to the music which she hears, however measured or far away.

REFRIGERATED BRAINS

See, people who make the number-one music hits, and commercials, and popular movies, and television shows, and game systems know something you don't: once you turn eleven and enter middle school, they're in charge.

They're in charge of your brain.

Many of the companies in charge of your brain are controlled by CEOs (short for *chief executive officers*) who are usually male and often white. Hey, nothing against white men here—I am, after all, one of them—but do you, as a middle school student who is not an old white man, want an old white man controlling your brain?

I hope not.

I *seriously* hope not.

But what these CEOs and their companies know is that you're going to watch the movies they make with the messages they choose are important; you're going to buy the clothes they make, even if they do reveal 97.6 percent of your flesh in the freezing winter; you're going to buy their newest game system and shoot 5,967 people dead during the course of Crazy Creepy Car Racing Game 47 and think it's awesome if you can kill more people than your friends; and you are, most definitely, going to listen to the lyrics of the songs they produce which tell you that if you're not in a relationship, *something is wrong with you!*

Basically, these companies think they've wrapped your brain in the plastic wrap your mom or dad uses to store leftovers in the fridge, and then these companies keep your plastic-wrapped brain in a huge refrigerator at their company warehouse. Then they laugh as they point at your brain, declaring, "We'll decide the meaning of life for this brain!"

A CONVERSATION WITH MR. BUTTMUNCHER

Okay, you're right. They don't *actually* have your literal brain in these company warehouses. But they're getting close. Trust me. Here's a conversation I had recently with the CEO of a huge company, one whose clothes you have probably purchased. To mask his real name, I will refer to him, in the most polite way possible, as Mr. Buttmuncher. Here's the conversation in full (I had a hidden recorder stuffed inside of a *huge* piece of buttery garlic bread when we talked):

Mr. Buttmuncher: So, Luke, what brings you to my office today?

Luke: The brains, Mr. Buttmuncher. I want to talk about the brains.

Mr. Buttmuncher: Er-uh—what brains? I don't know anything about brains, Luke, Really.

Luke: I know that you know that I know all about the brains, and I want to talk about those brains, **right now**.

Mr. Buttmuncher: Who sent you here?

Luke: My students did. I told them what you were doing to all the middle-school brains, and they demanded that I pay you a visit to ask you something. So I'm not leaving here until I ask it, Mr. Buttmuncher.

Mr. Buttmuncher: You ask your question, Luke, but then I'm calling security, and you're out of here faster than something really, really fast.

Luke: Fine.

Mr. Buttmuncher: Fine.

Luke: My question is this: Why do you do it? Why are you trying to control all these middle-school minds so that you can make gobs of money and buy seventeen houses?

Mr. Buttmuncher: Ha! You've wasted your question!

Luke: Why?

Mr. Buttmuncher: Because you've answered it yourself. I control all of these middle-school minds because it's **easy**; these middle schoolers are practically **begging** me to tell them what to wear, what to think, how to act, everything. So I tell them what to do, and they pay me for it. Well, their parents mostly pay me for it. But I'm getting stinking rich simply by helping them not think about who they really are. And it's so easy!

Luke: That's sick!

Mr. Buttmuncher: Hey, I didn't make up the system. I'm just great at playing the game! **(Evil laugh.)**

So that's the story behind the story. The many CEOs out there like Mr. Buttmuncher are like the space gnomes: they want to steal your brain just as much as the space gnomes want to steal all your garlic bread! So you've got to change the story, and *fast*. First off, you've got to start by taking back control of your brain.

The companies that own most middle school students' brains love telling you exactly what to wear, buy, watch, listen to, and think. How do they do this? They pay for advertisements on television; they put up huge posters in the mall; they pay singers a ton of money to sing about sex and drugs and how cool and fun both are to do, no matter how old you are.

Consider the mall. As you stroll by the stores, posters are plastered around you, shouting to you: *Look like me! Dress like me!* You're probably seeing a ton of posters of women dressed in super-tight or super-skin-showing clothes, and they're laughing gleefully as they hang on to a guy who's built like a truck. And the truck guys are looking tough and acting like they don't know what the word *emotion* means.

Or consider the billboards along highways. You can ride in the car and spot the same kinds of advertisements everywhere—half-naked gleeful women and chiseled emotionless men!

Or consider magazines. Consider movies. Consider commercials. The gleeful half-naked woman and the unfeeling buff man are surprisingly well traveled.

If you're just going through the mall, passing by billboards, or flipping through a magazine, these images are saying to your brain: *This is what's cool, home skillet. Word up, this is, like, the bomb. If you want ANYONE to respect you or think you're hot or cool or tough, then you better wear these clothes and have this body. Period.*

However, every time you actually think about these images and what they're really trying to get you to do, you take back your brain. Because when you *really question* the images, your brain might start to say stuff like: *Whoever decided that it was cool for a girl to wear skimpy clothes when it's freezing outside?* And your brain might also humbly suggest something like: *Whoever decided that guys are supposed to have, like, a thousand muscles on their shoulders and never seem emotional?*

Questions like these are dangerous, but not for you. These are exactly the kind of questions that the companies and their CEOs do *not* want you to ask—because when you start asking these questions, you begin to realize that the answers kind of don't make any sense. When you ask: *Who decided that THIS is what's cool?* you realize the answer is people who want to make money off of you not thinking for yourself.

When you ask these questions, the space gnomes get spooked. You're starting to find some of that caked dirt inside of you. You're taking a gooey, warm, fresh, buttery bite of garlic bread. And doing this drives the space gnomes absolutely bonkers. They might even come at you harder, stronger, faster. But if you keep asking questions, you find more and more of the caked dirt inside of you. And your mouth tastes more and more of the stunning garlic bread.

We don't have to be what you want us to be.

—Bill Russell, Basketball Hall of Fame inductee
who is taller than a fairy tale giant

The second thing you can do to start taking back some of your brain is to pause before you make a decision. You read that right. It's simple, but it can make a huge difference in your life as a middle school student.

Try it. The next time you have to make a decision—whether it's what kind of ice cream to get, what to say to the person you want to go out with, or whether or not to whisper that juicy rumor to your friend—just pause.

Once you've told yourself, "Self, pause! Stop!" then you're ready to complete the next step: count to ten slowly in your head. That's it. You can count in Spanish or another language if you like, especially if you need to practice it for class. Or you could even make up your own words for the numbers one through ten (although that sounds like an awful lot of work for a very simple step).

After you've counted to ten, something happens. Something so crazy and weird and cool and marvelous and mysteriously magical that if I just flat out told you what it was, you'd call me a liar.

But since I'm writing about thinking for yourself, I'm going to let you in on what happens when you pause and count to ten before you make a decision. However, be warned: what happens when you stop and count to ten before making a decision is actually kind of *freaky* and a little *gooey*.

10,000 GOOEY FRIENDS

Inside your brain (and my brain too!) are between 100 and 200 *billion* tiny (and gooey) neurons. Imagine a whole lot of really tiny balls that all have little sticks poking out of them, and you'll get the idea. These hundreds of billions of neurons all talk to each other because, hey, they're pretty dang friendly. In fact, each of them can make friends with about 10,000 other neurons. When they make friends (also called *synapses*), you make decisions.[2]

These tiny, poky-stick, gooey balls are making friends *every time you see something*—an image, a poster, a movie, an event, anything. This mob of gooey neurons start talking about the images with their other neuron friends. Say there's this image that gets people really excited, like a movie poster of a famous actress and actor, where she is tightly clothed and almost naked, and he is muscular, tough, and emotionless. Just looking at that image, without thinking much about it, will automatically create this massive mob of tens of thousands of neurons, all of them saying the same old thing: "Yeah, awesome poster! Let's have a party to celebrate this poster!"

But! (And a very big *but* here.)

When you suddenly stop and count to ten when you see the image or the poster or the movie, then you stop these neurons from making the same old 10,000 friends. You kind of dash in and break up the unthinking mob party. Here's how it works:

Your Neurons: Whoa, there's that image (again!) of the almost-naked, tightly clothed girl and the muscular, tough, emotionless guy! Yeah! So cool! So exciting! Pass it on!

Your Next 10,000 Neurons: We hear you! Yes! Yes! All hail half-naked women and tough guys!

You: Hold on, everyone. Wait . . . just . . . about . . . ten seconds . . .

Your Neurons: Whoa, wait? Really? Stop? Okay, if you say so . . .

Your Next 10,000 Neurons: Hey, Neurons—yeah, everyone—listen up! Memo in: we're holding on for ten seconds. Wait. Pass it on.

Now, while you're telling your neurons to wait—and counting to ten—you give your neurons a chance to think for themselves. And the *really* crazy thing is: when they start thinking for themselves, they make *new* friends. Instead of following the same old paths (called *synapses*), they start going down new paths and making new friends with loads of other neurons that they might never have met before, and then your gooey brain actually *changes*.[3]

I am totally serious. Your brain actually changes. This still kind of freaks me out a little bit. Plus, it keeps the space gnomes really confused because they have no idea how to figure out any of your garlic bread hiding spots (which drives them insane). When these new neuron-buddies are made, your changed brain thinks new thoughts, and those new thoughts grow stronger, and then *you become more who you want to be.*

One doesn't discover new lands without consenting to lose sight of the shore for a very long time.

—André Gide, Nobel Prize–winning author, and avid writer who kept a thirteen hundred page journal as a teen

So the good news is that you can then start deciding for yourself who you want to be. This is pretty cool stuff, because you'll find that you're smart, you have good ideas, and it feels stinking awesome to make a decision based on your own ideas rather than on the poster of the guy whose pectorals look like cannons and the woman whose chest looks like cannonballs. (By the way, who wants to let cannon people make decisions for them?)

The bad news is that making decisions for yourself is also hard work. It's hard, because your brain is actually thinking. It feels pretty smooth and easy to let an advertisement or a movie or a television show do the thinking for you. But if you do that, then your brain shrivels up like a raisin—and, hey, watch out or someone might eat it!

A RECYCLED WARDROBE?

There's one more thing you can do to start taking back your brain from that fridge in the company warehouse. You can stop shopping so frequently at the mall, stop buying the number-one songs on the chart, and stop trying to look like the guys and girls in commercials, movies, and huge posters.

Okay—I know what you're thinking about this. In fact, I know *exactly* what you're thinking about it, and I'll prove it to you. If you were in front of me right now, this is the conversation we would have (based on what you are thinking . . . right . . . now):

You: I was with you on all this stuff until you said, "Stop going to the mall." Luke, you're kind of a weirdo, man! This is crazy stuff, and I'm not reading any more of it. Shouldn't your book be, like, banned or something?

Me: Hi, You. Nice to have you here with me in my classroom as I write this book. Can I get you anything? A tall glass of milk? Some garlic bread? Anything? Anything at all?

You: No . . . no, thank you, Luke. I didn't come here to eat. I came to tell you that there's no way I'm going to stop shopping at the mall, and you're crazy. Plus, even if I wanted some milk and a nice fat slice of garlic bread, for real, how are you going to get it to me?

Me: Good point. Since you're not **technically** here with me, I guess I'd have to mail it to you. I'll use bubble wrap and lids so the milk won't spill. I'll overnight it to you—just leave your full name and address before you go.

You: Fine.

Me: Great!

You: But I am **so done** reading your book.

Me: Whoa, whoa, whoa! But you haven't even gotten to the really juicy stuff about love and relationships and going out and all of that. It's in the very next chapter! Trust me, just finish this chapter and get to the next chapter. You'll love it, I promise!

You: Fine. But I'm not reading any more of this chapter. I'm skipping ahead to chapter 4 for the juicy stuff right now.

Me: But how can you skip ahead? I mean, we're having this conversation right now. If you skip ahead, it will just be me writing back and forth between myself, and I don't want people thinking I'm **that** weird.

You: But you already are writing back and forth to yourself right now. Remember, I'm not really here, right?

Me: That's beside the point.

You: Then what is the point?

Me: So glad you asked! The point is this: if you keep shopping at the mall, purchasing the same clothes as everyone else, only buying the songs that are number one, and watching the same commercials and television shows—well, if you keep doing all that stuff, it's really hard to block the messages those CEOs and their companies are sending to your brain.

You: I'm falling asleep here, man, come on . . .

Me: Okay, think about it like this: say you decide to never, ever think of pink elephants again.

You: Okay, uh . . . I really don't get what you're trying to say . . .

Me: Well, if you decide you will never think of pink elephants **ever**, but then you have pink elephant wallpaper in your bedroom, and you use pink elephant toothpaste at night, and you have a pink elephant backpack, and you own a pink elephant that you keep in the backyard, it's going to be **really** hard to stop thinking of pink elephants because they're all around you.

You: So?

Me: So if you want to stop believing that you have to look, dress, and act a certain way, the more you stop letting your eyes see all those posters and movies, and the more you stop your ears from hearing the same lyrics about getting high, using guns, making bags of cash, or disrespecting your partner, well, the more you'll be able to think for yourself. It's kind of like cleaning out some space in your head for your own thoughts.

You: Okay, I get it. But if I don't buy clothes at the mall, where will I buy them?

Me: Okay, now you're probably really going to flip. But hear me out: a used clothing store.

You: Used what?

Me: A vintage clothing store. A consignment store. A thrift store that sells secondhand clothes— meaning, like, these clothes have been recycled.

You: Ewww!

Me: Not recycled like that sticky soda bottle in the recycling bin—more like, they've been worn by other people for a little while and then have been given away. You can buy tons of clothes really cheap. And you can usually find some pretty sweet stuff there. You don't have to buy all your clothes there—but just try going to the store once and see what it's like. Because when you walk through the doors of a used clothing store, trust me, there's no such thing as a CEO around making choices for you, and there are certainly no posters on the wall of cannon-pec men or cannonball-boob women. Instead, you really get to pick from all kinds of styles—and you can find something that's really . . . really . . . **you**.

You: Fine, I'll go, but only **once**.

Me: Deal.

You: Deal.

I'm really glad you and I had that little talk. In case you think I'm trying to get you to become a hippie or something, let me tell you straight out: I'm not! I just want you to see that there are other choices besides the ones you're constantly shown as the *only* choices. Movies, television shows, video games, giant posters in the mall— these aren't your only options for how to look, how to dress, and what to think. I promise: there are a whole bunch of other ways to live than these!

You can do with music what you just agreed to do with clothes. Instead of always buying the number-one hit, check out your town's public library. It has an *amazing* CD collection. I guarantee it. I promise. Go and ask the librarian to see the collection, and *you can check out any CD for free.* Just flip through and see the covers of the CDs, read the names of the songs on the back, and try taking out a few that reach in and tug on a few thousand of those beautiful, gooey neurons in your beautiful, gooey brain. Just like Shooting Star at the beginning of the chapter, you might discover a new favorite group or song!

So you stuck with me through chapter 3. Whew—I was worried for a few moments there, but I'm glad you made it. Now you're almost into the juiciest chapter of them all: chapter 4, the L-O-V-E chapter.

But before we launch ahead into that strange and beautiful territory, I want you to do something for me. Please. It won't take too long (but here's a warning: it may involve a conversation with your parents, or guardians, or siblings), and it's really important.

EXERCISE
Have a Chat with Your Five-Year-Old Self

Find a picture of yourself when you were five years old. Find any picture and then tape it right into your journal (if you have one), or onto the wall above your desk, or above your bed. If you can't find a single picture of yourself (or if the space gnomes have stolen them all to begin the transport process of your DNA to their home planet), then draw yourself at five. (Don't worry about artistic judgment here. Stick figures rock.)

Now, stare at the eyes of this tiny little human being. Notice how super cool you were then. Next, (making sure no one else is around), I want you to talk to this five-year-old human. Tell this five-year-old that *it's going to be okay.* Tell this five-year-old that the stuff you cared about then still matters. Tell this five-year-old that you could still fly to the moon; you could still fight fires; you could still leap high into the air in your leotard. You *can.* See the eyes of this five-year-old and remember that back then, you didn't care what the most popular clothes or music were.

Now, below your picture (or on a paper that you can tape up next to your picture), write in really thick marker/pen/garlic bread butter ink:

The five-year-old inside me matters.

Because it's true. There's a part of you that still doesn't care what brand your clothes are or what the word **popularity** means. There's someone inside you who wants to dream dreams, wonder, and **do** something beautiful, bold, and adventurous. Look at that five-year-old's eyes. *Those eyes are still yours.* That five-year-old is still wildly alive inside of you.

4

THE MOVES MAKE THE MAN; THE LOOKS MAKE THE LADY (NOT!)

Here's where you see what love, armpit sweat, going out, crying, and individuality have in common. Hint: it's not that they are types of pizza toppings.

A STORY ABOUT A TOUGH GUY

As a middle school teacher, I know for a fact that some of the coolest, seemingly toughest guys and girls in middle school have very different emotional insides than the tough exteriors that they show the world. I'll never forget one of these guys, and I keep him forever in my heart. (Not *actually* in my heart, though. He would have to be, like, a really, really tiny human being to fit inside my heart. Plus, it would be really bloody in there.)

I'll call him Philbert so I don't embarrass him. Philbert was the kind of guy you're probably afraid of. Right now, a boy like Philbert is probably enrolled in your middle school. He could be looking over your shoulder this very moment. Maybe he's flipping your book over as you're reading—

Whoa! You okay? That wasn't cool—messing with your book like that.

Philbert was a big guy, kind of like Goliath, who slammed the locker door in my face when I was starting middle school. Philbert was always tough and cool on the outside. He made sure other kids were afraid of him, and he always seemed to have a girl on his arm. For a long time, I tried getting through to Philbert—because I knew there had to be real emotion under that tough exterior, all that I'm-so-cool-you-can't-even-walk-down-the-same-hallway-as-me stuff. But no matter what, Philbert wasn't about to let me break into his neat little way of living through middle school.

Until.

One day, word got around to us teachers that Philbert and his buddy were standing at the top of the stairwell at the end of a long hallway on the second floor of the middle school. When the bell rang and students passed from one class to another, Philbert and his buddy would act like giants, shoving kids around, making fun of students as they passed, and hooting at the girls. Basically, they were terrifying a lot of students.

This made me mad. It takes an awful lot to get Mr. Reynolds mad—but this did it. Some other teachers and I pulled Philbert and his buddy into my classroom. I set out two chairs for them to sit across from me, and I just stared at them for about a full minute.

If you ever want to make people squirm, just look at them. I mean, really look at them. Just stare into their eyes. Most people don't ever look at other people's eyes for more than a second or two.

I stared hard at Philbert and his buddy. When I spoke, my tone was serious and strong, with that don't-give-me-any-crap tinge to it. I said a lot to Philbert and his buddy that day. I reamed them out in my almost-shouting voice and gave them some serious consequences.

But I also said just one thing to Philbert that showed me what was really going on inside. I looked him in the eye and said, "I know there are people at home who don't believe in you. I know you think a man is supposed to be tough and never feel fear. I'm here to tell you *that's not true.* And that's not who you really are." I waited for a moment, and I looked him in the eye and said again, "That's *not* who you really are."

And Philbert cried. The tears started rolling down his face, and I had to remind myself that I was his teacher. I couldn't run over to him and give him a big hug. But I did promise that I would try to help him see another way.

Now, I wish I could tell you that Philbert left the classroom that day and was an emotional, sensitive guy forever and ever. I wish I could tell you that his buddy respected him and also began crying whenever something struck him as sad.

No.

Philbert still struggled, and he still sometimes did some mean stuff to others. As did his buddy. I didn't transform Philbert into the kindest kid on the planet, but Philbert had a moment when he let what was inside come up to the *outside.* You've got to be willing to look at the inside. The good news and the hard news is this: Love is about bringing the inside to the outside. Love is about sharing the life that is *really* inside of you so you can talk and act like the person you really are—not who you think you're supposed to be.

> ## We have to dare to be ourselves, however frightening or strange that self may prove to be.
> —May Sarton, poet and novelist, who believed the pen is mightier than the sword (or the light saber)

The idea that boys don't cry is only *one* of the many lies when it comes to how girls and boys are *supposed* to think and act in middle school. I have found all six lies about love in middle school. Let's dig our fingers into these lies, throw them up in the air, and then slice them with gargantuan fingernail clippers. It will drive the space gnomes crazy—come on!

THE LIES ABOUT LOVE

So. You're in sixth, seventh, or eighth grade now (or about to start one of those grades). So far in your life, you probably haven't been terribly concerned with falling in love. Maybe you've always thought of romance and falling in love as dis-gusting. But now . . . well . . . now, something all weird and tingly is happening inside you when you look at that boy you've known for years or that girl who sits next to you in class. Your face gets all hot, and your armpits start pouring gallons and gallons of sweat, like they're mini, sweat-producing Niagara Falls. And forget about being yourself around someone you like—impossible! It's hard enough to even remember your own name. (By the way, this is the reason boys don't say much around someone they like. It's not that they're so cool and tough, but rather that their heads are saying, *Holy crap holy crap holy crap, it's Jessie! Right there in front of me! Quick, stop talking and look tough . . . look cool . . . look strong and silent!*)

So before getting into some tips on how to survive middle school in the midst of all these crazy-strong feelings you're having, let's begin by debunking a few things that you might think are true. The following things are *absolutely false*. So in other words, the list below contains statements that are 100 percent, *entirely, completely, utterly, overwhelmingly NOT TRUE*:

Lie #1: The way you look is all that matters when it comes to love.

Lie #2: If you're not going out with someone in middle school, you're not cool.

Lie #3: Love is about needing someone else so badly that you can't live without them.

Lie #4: Boys don't have emotions.

Lie #5: Girls are only attractive if they dress in skimpy or tight clothes.

Lie #6: It's now or never.

Just in case you forgot, I want to remind you before we go on that all six statements above are *wrong*. Instead of believing the above things, though, what are you supposed to think when you're in middle school? After all, the movies you watch and the songs you listen to and the posters and commercials and everything else say the above things are *true*. So either I am lying or all those other people are lying.

Okay, you may find this hard to believe, but all those other people are lying.

Let me explain why all those statements are wrong and all those other people are lying. Let's start with the first lie and work our way on from there. I promise I'll throw in some juicy stories from my own life, and from the lives of my students, and from the lives of the space gnomes.

Lie #1: The way you look is all that matters when it comes to love.

I know, you've seen it a thousand times, right? In every romance movie, the guy is muscular, popular, and has a face that looks like it was chiseled from stone. And the girl is so hot, she makes really, really, really hot garlic bread look frozen. And of course, they end up falling madly in love with one another—largely because of their respective hotness (*sizzle!*).

First of all, the people you're watching fall in love don't actually even look like that themselves. Their faces have been plastered with makeup and thick layers of fake-skin-type stuff so that you're not even seeing what's really there. They, too, get pimples (sometimes the size of mountains); they, too, would have sweat stains (if they didn't change their clothes every five minutes while filming); and they, too, get rashes and feel overweight (and might even have, like, six toes on one foot or something). They have nose hair and thigh hair (and fingernail hair and hair on top of their hair). They're human, just like you (even though the big screen and the posters convince us that they're not).

(Note: The space gnomes actually *are* hairless, and they are quite angry about it. Hair is very desirable for space gnomes, and once they get all the garlic bread they can from us, I'm betting they'll move on to hair theft.)

Second, people who *do* look even close to that perfectly perfect generally don't end up very happy in real life. Have you ever noticed that, in real life, the hottest movie stars end up getting approximately 5.67 divorces by the time they're thirty years old?

Third, if you find yourself continually drawn to people only because of the way they look, there's a good chance you might miss the real people beneath those looks! The outer skin is pretty much just the outer crust of the garlic bread. It doesn't really show anything about all the amazing stuff and softness of the inside! And there's no way to tell how much garlicky goodness and buttery freshness is all waiting on the inside if we simply stare at the outside! Trying to figure out what's on the inside by studying the crust isn't going to tell us anything except, well, what the crust looks like. The depth is all on the inside. The character is all on the inside. And you want to see that person within!

Character, not circumstance, makes the man.
—Booker T. Washington, African-American speaker, author, educator, and activist from the late 1800's to the early 1900's

I had one student—I'll call him Romeo Basketball—who was madly in love with a girl—I'll call her Shockwave. Romeo Basketball believed that Shockwave was the hottest girl ever to exist on Planet Earth (though he wasn't sure he could make the claim for the universe, not having been outside his home planet). Romeo Basketball believed that if he just got Shockwave to go out with him, his life would be perfect. Many days, after school, while he was supposed to be finishing homework, Romeo Basketball would tell me about his love for Shockwave and would wish longingly that she was his girlfriend.

Well, you guessed it. Eventually, Shockwave agreed to go out with Romeo Basketball. And for a while, the two of them were like peanut butter and marshmallow fluff, or like roses grown off of the same vine, or like two fluffy buttery roses when smushed together, or like any other two things that really, really couldn't get enough of one another.

But then they started arguing about tons of things. Romeo Basketball thought Shockwave didn't come to enough of his basketball games. Shockwave thought Romeo Basketball was flirting with other girls. The list grew and grew, until finally, they started hating one another. They each took turns dumping one another—six or seven times over the course of a week—and then they called it quits for good. Fortunately for me, I had both Romeo Basketball and Shockwave in the same class, and while I was trying to teach them all about iambic pentameter and rhyme scheme, their spiteful eyes just glared back and forth at one another.

Needless to say—as Romeo Basketball later confessed to me after school one day (when he was supposed to be doing homework)—he'd only wanted to go out with Shockwave because of her looks.

If that is the only exciting draw about someone else, then there is a whole human being that is ignored! Getting to know who a person is beneath the skin—and letting other people get to know us beneath our skin—is how real love can begin.

For both Shockwave and Romeo Basketball, imagine what would have happened if they'd been friends *first*—if they had taken time to talk about what they think, like, laugh about, hope for, believe in, and are scared of, or how they feel about space gnomes, or how much garlic bread they could eat in a single meal? All of this would have helped them get deeper than their crusts. And remember: that's what we *really* want to share with each other—not just our outsides but also our insides.

Lie #2: If you're not going out with someone in middle school, you're not cool.

Whoa, whoa, whoa! This is totally untrue! First of all, let's investigate what the words *going out* actually mean. They *seem* to mean that you date another person—that you actually go out with said person to the movies, or out for dinner at a nice restaurant, or go out to a park for a romantic picnic. If that definition is anything close to being right, then there's kind of no such thing as "going out" with someone in middle school. Why? Because that's usually not what having a boyfriend or a girlfriend even means in middle school.

Case in point: my six-day romance when I was in the seventh grade. I'll call my six-day girlfriend Sixer to avoid any embarrassing recognition on her part, if she happens to be reading this book right now. (However, Megan, if you are reading this book now, it would be somewhat strange,

since we both left middle school almost twenty years ago!) There was no such thing back then as a cell phone, or instant messaging, or texting, or Snapchatting, or anything of that sort. So I did it the old-fashioned, brave, courageous way: I wrote a short note and gave it to one of my friends, who gave it to one of his friends, who gave the note to one of Sixer's friends, who then passed it to another friend, from whom a teacher took the note and ripped it up.

Then, I wrote *another* note, and gave it to a friend, who gave it to a friend, who gave it to a friend, who slipped the note through a slat in Sixer's locker.

I can't remember exactly what the note said, although if I had to really work hard to try to envision what my seventh-grade hand nervously wrote on that page, it probably went something like this:

Dear Sixer,
What up, home slice?! You are so hot that when I walk past you in the hallways, I sometimes feel like I should be carrying around a fire extinguisher with me, like under my shirt or something (you know, because of how hot you are—so hot that the hallway could probably burst into flames and everything).
Anyway. Will you go out with me?

Yours Truly,
Luke Reynolds

I'm not sure if that was *exactly* the note that I wrote so many years ago, but I think it's pretty darn close. If you want to try to do some sleuthing, you can probably contact Sixer using the following email: Megan.Shipler.Middle.School.Six.Days@superfastemail connection.com.

Well, the rest, as they say, was history. Sixer wrote me a note and then passed it along the secretive chain until it reached me. Her reply was, after a series of sentences, ultimately, *Yes*.

So we started going out. But we never technically went out anywhere. We merely moved to opposite sides of the hall when we passed one another between classes, and got red in the face when someone mentioned the other person's name, and once in a great while, gave a quick hug to each other before rushing home so that we could talk on the phone.

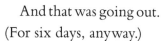

And that was going out. (For six days, anyway.)

When I started teaching middle school students like yourself, I wondered if going out still meant the same thing. Thus, I decided I would bring up the subject one day after we had read "When You Are Old," a poem about love by W. B. Yeats. (By the way, this is hands down the most remarkable poem ever written about love. In case you want to read and memorize it forever, try Googling "When You Are Old poem." I even recited the poem to my girlfriend, Jennifer—who would later become my wife—the night I first said those garlic-bread-type-magical words: *I love you.* And even though my mom called twice while I was reciting the poem, it was still pretty cool.)

My students told me that, yes, going out was pretty much the same as the way *I* described how it was when I was in middle school, so long ago. (Except now, instead of talking on the phone, it's texting and Snapchatting!) And as I watched my students "go out" with one another over the course of my teaching, I learned that indeed it hasn't changed much!

So if going out with someone is really not that much different from eating way too many McDonald's french fries and then feeling kind of bloated and awkward, then why not realize that you don't have to go out with someone to be cool in middle school? You don't need anyone else to prove that. (Which brings us to Lie #3.)

Lie #3: Love is about needing someone else so badly that you can't live without them.

Is not!

Is not!

Is not!

There was a very popular movie released some years ago. You probably haven't seen it. However, it's a good example of what I mean here about not needing someone else so badly that you can't live without them. The movie is *Jerry Maguire*, starring Tom Cruise and Renée Zellweger. At one point in the film, Cruise's character looks at Zellweger's character (serenaded with Hollywood romance music playing) and says, "You complete me."

If you think this is super romantic, then you're like I used to be and like most of the middle school students I teach. (And the high school students I used to teach believed this lie too!) But the truth is: you're a complete human being just as you are. That's right. You're not some part of a puzzle that needs another puzzle piece to fit into you to make you worthwhile or complete. Your value doesn't depend on someone else, no matter how madly in love you are with that someone.

If it did, then you would be this incomplete person doing half of everything until you found Mr. or Ms. Right. You'd only eat half your breakfast. You'd do half of your work. You'd finish only half of all the sentences you'd speak. You'd watch half of a movie and then suddenly stop the movie and do something else (but then only finish half of that too). You'd start to make some garlic bread, but only end up putting butter and garlic on half of it, baking it for half of the time necessary, and taking out a—yup—half-baked loaf of garlic bread. You'd sleep only half of the night. You'd brush only half of your teeth. You'd cut every dollar you ever got in half (and then you'd have a heck of a time trying to buy anything with your half dollars, but then again, you'd only make it halfway to any of the stores anyway)! You'd even only get halfway dressed in the morning, and that could be pretty awkward (not to mention cold, if it's winter).

And hey, who wants to live only half a life? If you decide that being only half of yourself is really the best way, then you're going to miss out on a whole heck of a lot of other cool stuff too (besides simply seeing the ends of movies and having all of your teeth be clean). You'll also miss chances for new friendships, new hobbies and interests that could develop, new ways of seeing yourself, and maybe even a really funny joke, or the teacher farting, or just a *full* loaf of fresh, warm, fully baked garlic bread. (By the way, if you choose *not* to halve your way through middle school and you end up getting the full loaf of garlic bread—save me a piece! I'm coming over!)

Once, a female student told me that her boyfriend had dumped her because, and this is a direct quote from her: "I'm not making him feel good enough about himself." My student was in tears, telling me that she wished she'd just worked harder to make him feel the way he wanted to feel—in other words, to *complete him.* Of course, I wanted to grab the brain of this student and shake said brain and say, "No, no, no! Don't you see that he doesn't even know what the heck he's talking about?! The way he feels is up to him—it's not something you have power over. It isn't your responsibility!"

But if I had grabbed my student's brain and started shaking it, surely I would have been fired. So what did I do? I calmly asked her if she thought he was really right about that. When my student said yes, she thought he was exactly right, I asked her if she really, really, *really (really?!)* thought he was right about that. Then she thought for a moment (I'm not sure if she counted to ten), and she said, "Well, maybe . . . not?"

"Bingo!" I said.

"Bingo, what?" she replied.

"Bingo, *maybe not!*" I shouted joyfully.

We went on to discuss something deeper: that love doesn't ever ask you to complete or fill in another person, like you are some kind of puzzle. Instead, love asks you to care for, encourage, challenge, and see another person for who they are and who they're striving to become. A person in love should be more like a loaf of garlic bread than a puzzle. You can eat garlic bread totally on its own—without pasta, without sauce, without even a drink—and it is still amazing. Fresh, warm, and amazing. But you can *also* enjoy garlic bread *with* any of these other things, and these other things can enhance the garlic bread. Yes! But on its own, garlic bread is still pretty awesome. (Which is, of course, why the space gnomes are constantly trying to steal it.)

We don't see things as they are; we see them as we are.

—Anaïs Nin, twentieth-century author who pushed past traditional standards (and was awesome!)

So if you had to choose, would you rather enjoy a full loaf of fresh, warm garlic bread or try to complete a puzzle with only half the pieces, constantly waiting to see if someone else was going to show up with the rest of the pieces?

You're worthwhile just as you are.

You're complete as you are.

You're *you*. And that is enough.

Lie #4: Boys don't have emotions.

Hey, I'm a boy. Okay, fine, I'm a man. But I still often act like a boy. Sometimes, when I'm teaching and people walk into my classroom, they can't really tell if I am, in fact, the teacher or if I'm a giant seventh grader merely wearing a shirt and tie and growing a beard.

My point is this: I'm male, and let me tell you, *I have emotions!* Ask my wife. Ask my sons. I cry. I weep, in fact. When I read a beautiful book, I cry. Just before I sat down to write the exact words you are reading right now, I was reading a book by Kathryn Erskine called *The Absolute Value of Mike*, and I got to this incredible scene, and I just started crying, right there while I sat on the toilet while I was reading. (Yes, I often read while sitting on the toilet. You should try it sometime if you haven't already. Researchers argue that the human brain can be incredibly focused and is often creatively freed while sitting on the toilet. Try studying for your next test while you're sitting on the porcelain throne.[4])

When I watch a movie that's about truth and love and passion, I cry. Like *Amazing Grace*. I've seen it ten times with my wife, Jennifer. It's about a man named William Wilberforce, who destroyed the evil of the slave trade in England in the 1800s. I weep every time I watch the end of that film.

When one of my sons comes up to me and throws his arms around me and calls me Daddy, you'd better believe my eyes aren't dry! Hey, even just thinking about some of these things is making me get a little teary eyed. Do you happen to have a box of tissues nearby? Yeah? Could I snag one of them?

Thank you.

And since I'm male, and I cry, I promise you this: all those boys in your middle school right now cry too. As one of *my* old teachers used to say, I'm as serious as a heart attack. Remember Philbert from the story at the start of our chapter?

Guys, if you're reading this now, then you already know deep down: you weren't built to be some kind of robot who's always tough and doesn't show emotion and just acts cool. That's called being phony and fake. And I know there are a lot of role models who are phony and fake. But that's not who *you* are. You were meant to be something much more real than that. You were meant to show emotion, to be honest, and to realize that being a man doesn't mean hiding your heart.

My grandfather, Harold Fenton, is now ninety-six years old—and the man still seems tougher than a thousand nails all melted together and forged into one massively sharp nail. Yet, I still remember the exact moment when, ten years ago, I sat across the dinner table from him, and he was telling me about his last moments with my grandmother. She had died of Alzheimer's, and my grandfather looked me in the eye and said the words, "I miss her so much, it hurts," and he cried. And he cried. And he cried. My grandfather had built forty-seven houses and owned his own construction business—and I had heard stories of how hard he was on the guys who worked for him—and yet watching him weep in that moment, I saw the emotion that lies underneath all that toughness. I saw the raw love inside of my grandfather.

Girls, if you're reading this, understand that boys are going to try to act tough in front of you and pretend they don't get scared or sad. But they do. Just like you. I did when I was in middle school. (And I do now too.) And all the guys I know admit this too. And the boys I teach in seventh grade—many like Philbert— show me this every year too.

Lie #5: Girls are only attractive if they dress in skimpy or tight clothes.

Ladies, any guy who wants to go out with you because of the way you dress, well, that guy isn't worth a crumb of a loaf of garlic bread. Okay, I know I'm being harsh here, but it's the truth. Girls and guys, you might feel some wacky bodily changes when you look at certain parts of each other. But getting someone to go out with you is about *a lot* more than wacky bodily changes!

A student I taught in my seventh-grade class many years ago always wore what felt comfortable and right for her. And this was awesome because she was never freezing in the wintertime, and while other girls in class shivered, she could learn peacefully. But this student, who we will call Studentia, really wanted to go out with someone. She desperately wanted a boy to ask her to dance at one of the school dances (no one had asked her at the first two dances). Studentia desperately wanted someone to notice her and say she was beautiful and write her a note that began, *Dear Studentia, You rock!*

But no one did.

How do I know this?

Because one day after class, Studentia and one of her friends stayed after school to help out with a student anthology our class was building. Each student was writing a story for the anthology, and we were going to sell the books in front of the local grocery store and send the money to a very awesome organization called Women for Women International.

While we were printing out copies of the stories and getting them into their right places in the manuscript, Studentia said to her friend, "I really want a guy to ask me to dance. No one has asked me to dance at the first two dances. And I really want someone to write me a note that says, *Dear Studentia, You rock!*" She waited a moment, collated some pages, and then said, "Maybe I've got to show some skin."

Of course, I wanted to yell out: "No! Dress the way that feels comfortable and warm to you, Studentia!" But I didn't. I bit my tongue. (Ouch, biting your tongue actually does hurt. A lot.) Luckily, Studentia's friend told her this: "You don't have to change the way you are to get someone to like you." (Home run!)

The second half of the year went by. No one asked Studentia to dance. No one wrote her a note that said, *Dear Studentia, You rock!* And the year ended.

But then this crazy thing happened. Three years later, I got an email from Studentia, and the essence of the email, pretty much, was this: Someone was asking Studentia to dance. Someone was writing her notes that said, *You rock!* And she hadn't changed who she was, or dressed to show more skin, in order to get this guy to like her. Studentia told me, in her email, that the guy actually wrote (in one of his many notes) that what he appreciated most about Studentia was that *she was who she was*, and that she didn't try to be like everyone else.

It takes a smart woman to fall in love with a good man.

—Sadie & Bessie Delany, civil rights activists and coauthors
of *Having Our Say*

It may take time, but waiting for someone who appreciates who you really are is worth it. (Plus, you'll be a lot warmer in the winter.)

In the meantime, you can get to know the guys who you might not normally choose to get to know. You can get to know yourself too. You can get into music and movies and writing and sports and dance and art and see who you really are and who you really want to be. And you just might find that when you're seeking the stuff that makes you feel really alive and excited, there are guys and ladies who are seeking the very same things too.

Lie #6: It's now or never.

This lie gets into pretty much everything in middle school—and in society too! If you look around you, you're constantly being told that if you don't buy something during the sale (*now!*), you'll never be able to get it at that price again (*never!*). If you don't act a certain way *now*, you'll *never* get friends and be popular. If you don't do what other people want you to do *now*, then you'll *never* amount to anything in this world.

Everything mentioned above is beyond fake. In fact, it's so fake that we need to invent a new word to describe the immense load of crap we just encountered up above. (By the way, can you smell the stench coming from those lies above? Man! That stuff stinks! Let's get to the next paragraph, just to have a few more words between that smell and us.)

Ah—much better. Chances are, anything in life that is *now or never* is probably designed to trick you into doing something that really isn't all that good for you. Whatever it is, it probably won't help you feel any better about yourself, and it certainly won't take away any pain you feel or make you a better person. Because good things take time. Good things generally grow more like trees than bubbles.

Have patience, heart.

—Homer, incredibly old (actually, now dead) Greek who wrote
The Odyssey

Trees take in water, sunlight, nutrients (okay, you get the point), and over the course of *years*, they develop into huge, strong things that you couldn't push over even if you tried. (Trust me, before writing this section of the book, I was outside pushing against a big tree as hard as I could, and the thing wouldn't budge. People walking past me thought I was crazy, but I just yelled back, "I'm testing a hypothesis!") If you planted a tree and then looked at it every day, it probably wouldn't look a darn bit different to you. But by the time you graduated high school, went off to college, and then came home, you'd look at that tree you planted and say, "Holy crap! That thing is huge!"

A bubble is the opposite. The thing puffs up huge right away—it stretches out large and looks wonderful in about 1.3 seconds. But then, by 2.4 seconds, it's popped.

Gone.

End of story.

If you're starting to think about what love is really all about (and you probably are, if you're anything like my students, or like me when I was in middle school), then remember this: Love is always more like a tree than a bubble. Love is always about patience rather than a now-or-never mentality. If any guys or girls try to convince you otherwise, blow a bunch of bubbles in their faces. Then, if they still don't get it, take them outside and tell them to try to push a tree over. I'm pretty sure that'll teach them.

(By the way, before doing the above things to someone who is trying to make you do something with a now-or-never mentality, it might help to explain what the bubbles and trees really mean.)

THE TRUTHS ABOUT LOVE

To conclude, instead of restating the super-cool, death-defying, gravity-rejecting points from this chapter, I think it would be wiser for us to check out the *opposites* of the six lies we discussed when it comes to love (and life).

Here they are, the Six Truths About Love:

Truth #1: When it comes to love, what matters most is who you are.

Truth #2: You're cool because of who you are, not who you're with.

Truth #3: Love is about realizing that you are complete on your own—no puzzle piece!

Truth #4: Boys do have emotions!

Truth #5: The way girls dress has nothing to do with being loved.

Truth #6: Love is about patience and growth (a tree, not a bubble).

EXERCISE
Finding Five

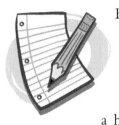 Before you leave the land of love, I'd like you to take a moment to draw a tree. Seriously. You know that you miss drawing trees from when you were three. Remember? You started drawing a house and then added a couple of trees next to it? Here's your chance to do that again! Yes!

Draw a tree right in your journal, or on a piece of blank paper, or on your belly. Now, inside the tree trunk, write five things you hope people will see about you *that have nothing to do with your body.*

Okay, I'm not trying to make you think you don't have a body. (I know, after all, that you are not simply a big collection of neurons walking around leaving gooey neuron trails because the space gnomes have stolen your body along with all of your garlic bread. I know this *has not* happened because, hey, you've already read about using your brain to make good decisions for your body in the previous chapters! You've already begun battling the space gnomes, so I know for a *fact* that they haven't stolen your garlic bread and your body!) But it's important to understand that if you *really* want someone to love you, then you want someone to see things about you that have nothing to do with your body. Our bodies change every single day. (Actually, every single second. Right now, one of your nose hairs just grew a tiny, tiny, tiny amount. Oh! It just grew again! Awesome!) You want someone to appreciate you for the things about you that don't change every single second.

Are you kind? Are you brave? Are you silly?

Let that tree-loving part of you draw, and let that self-loving part of you, well, *love.*

5

IS MIDDLE SCHOOL THE *TITANIC*? NO, BUT HERE'S AN ICEBERG TO THINK ABOUT ere's where you see what massive mountains of ice floating on the sea, pain, shovels, and *The Karate Kid* all have in common. Hint: it's *not* that each of these things is great to snuggle with while falling asleep.

A STORY ABOUT A QUIET KID

Every day, Shadowboxer came into my classroom, took his seat in the back row, and never said a word. Through every silly joke, every strange activity, and every novel that we read in class, Shadowboxer never even cracked a smile, or asked to use the bathroom, or talked to someone next to him. Thing is, though, he didn't necessarily look *sad* or *angry*, or like he had swallowed a whole potato in one gulp. Nothing like that. Shadowboxer just seemed . . . *quiet*. And surely, there are students in middle school who just like being quiet. And that's okay!

But then we started doing some partner projects, and Shadowboxer would quietly ask if he could work alone. Or others in the class—noticing that Shadowboxer could draw a pretty sweet doodle—asked him to be in their groups to work on a project. Shadowboxer always shook his head from side to side—*no*—without saying a word.

And so most of that year passed. I tried, as often as possible, to get Shadowboxer to talk in class, to talk after

class, to talk *anytime*. I even designed one entire lesson *just* for Shadowboxer: the goal was for students to be as distracted and *not* paying attention to the teacher as possible—to have as many side conversations as possible. Yeah!

But Shadowboxer paid perfect attention, his eyes straight toward the front of the room. Silent. Watching.

Fast forward to about one month before the end of the year. Students were writing in their journals in class, responding to the question: What is your greatest pain or your greatest joy? I looked up from my own journal and saw Shadowboxer writing like it was *the last chance on Earth to use paper as a device for recording thoughts before it all disappeared.*

Journal time ended, and we began to move on to the next part of our class. But then—what was that? *What was that?* WHAT WAS THAT?! Shadowboxer's hand was raised. And it stayed up. I wanted to take a picture right then and there, but instead I called out, "Yes, Shadowboxer?"

"Can I share mine?" Shadowboxer asked.

I almost choked. Then, after finishing almost choking, I replied, "Sure, that sounds great."

Shadowboxer proceeded to read two pages of writing out loud to the class that told us of his problems at home—that his dad and mom had been fighting *a lot* and saying really mean, nasty words to each other. And in one of the fights, they had decided that the father should leave home, and he did, and he stayed away from home. And then his parents got a divorce. And then Shadowboxer's heart had broken.

And as I listened, *my* heart was breaking.

He finished reading and quietly closed his journal. When a couple kids nearby put their hands on Shadowboxer's shoulders and said stuff like, "Thanks for sharing that, man," I knew those students felt similarly and were probably going through parental fighting and problems at home too. The running refrain in my own head was, *I never knew.*

THE THING ABOUT ICEBERGS . . .

Have you seen *Titanic* with Leonardo DiCaprio and Kate Winslet? It was big when I was in high school. I remember Celine Dion's song from the movie, "My Heart Will Go On," blasting through our school cafeteria and at school dances. Every time I hear the word *Titanic*, I think of nervously asking a girl to dance rather than a really huge ship that sank.

In case you don't know the story, or haven't seen the movie, here it is in a nutshell: The Titanic was a massive ship that set sail from London to New York—the biggest passenger ship that had ever attempted to venture across the Atlantic Ocean at that time. It was famously said of the ship that nothing could sink it. One night, the ship hit a massive iceberg in the middle of the ocean. It sank. End of story.

The really freaky thing about icebergs is this: only about 10 percent of their entire mass can be seen above the surface of the water.[5] So if you're swimming along in the middle of the ocean and come across an iceberg, and you think, *Hey, it's not really THAT big,* you'd be completely wrong. (By the way, don't go swimming in the middle of the ocean, especially if you want to make it to high school.)

So above the water, icebergs still look big, but not monstrous. Below the water, they are bigger than blue whales on steroids.

Everything has its wonders, even darkness and silence.

—Helen Keller, deaf and blind woman who radically changed education and people's perceptions

The reason I'm telling you all of this is because icebergs have an awful lot to do with middle school. In fact, every student I've ever met—including myself, even though I didn't know it at the time—has been an iceberg. You got it: all of my students have been massive chunks of ice just floating around in the ocean of middle school. And most of us remain icebergs our whole lives. Like Shadowboxer, most of us have hard (or good) stuff that we keep inside because it's terrifying to talk about, or because we're afraid of what people will think, or because we don't know *how* to let certain parts of ourselves out.

By the way, the space gnomes absolutely *love* it when we see ourselves and each other only by the tips of our iceberg selves. They go bonkers for this kind of thing. Because if we're busy studying the surfaces of each other and our lives, those stealthy space gnomes can sneak below the surface totally undetected (using their state-of-the-art space gnome scuba gear) and rob us without our even being aware of it! Meanwhile, we stare at the surface in fear and wonder what's making the bubbles from below. (Hint: the state-of-the-art scuba gear that the space gnomes wear has incredibly long flippers that make masses of bubbles.)

WHAT YOU SEE IS *NOT* WHAT YOU GET

I've taught students who seemed one way on the surface but on the inside were totally different. I've taught students who seemed like they had it all together but later shared that they were being bullied or taunted. I've taught students who dressed like they were fashion models and were thinner than was healthy but later shared that they felt they were way overweight. I've had students who acted tough and cool but then later shared that they cry themselves to sleep at night.

I'm not saying that everything is fake in middle school. No! There's a lot of fun, friendship, and joy to go around that is surely genuine. But when you see people acting a certain way—or find *yourself* acting a certain way—remember the icebergs. Remember that much of a person in middle school is way below the surface.

So even if someone seems like they have it all together, they might not.

If someone seems like they're beautiful and perfect, it's possible they don't actually feel this way.

If someone is having an awful day, there's probably a big reason beneath the surface that you just can't see.

I grew up wishing I could be like other people . . .
but all along . . . I was toughening up and learning,
all in the quest of becoming the me
I was meant to grow into.
—Anna Staniszewski, novelist and picture book author
who wields wit, warmth, and wonder

All of this doesn't excuse those kids who are mean or do hurtful things to others, but knowing this does help to deal with it. It helps to realize that a lot of life doesn't get airtime, and the things that do are often the 10 percent that lies above the surface, not the deep stuff that's really beneath.

When you see a really quiet kid in middle school, sure, that kid may just have swallowed a whole pizza or potato in one gulp. Or that kid may just be quiet—and that's okay! You may be that quiet kid, and that's okay. But, like Shadowboxer, there may be stuff underneath the 10 percent that's worth asking about, worth connecting with, worth sharing.

WHAT HAPPENED WITH SHADOWBOXER

A couple of weeks after Shadowboxer read his journal out loud to the class, he stayed after school one day to tell me that he loved the movie *The Karate Kid*. Just that.

"It's your favorite? What makes you love it so much?" I asked Shadowboxer.

"Everything," he replied, then went quiet.

"What part of everything is your favorite part?" I asked.

Shadowboxer looked up and then back at his feet, moved his feet around, then looked up again. "It's like, Daniel is this kid who seems totally out of place, and his family life kind of stinks, but then . . . but then, it's like the karate is inside him all along, you know what I mean? Like it was just *always there*, and he just had to, kind of, find it."

"I know exactly what you mean," I said.

And guess what movie we watched in class next?

EXERCISE
Seven Things People Don't See about YOU

Okay, try this. Today, something bad happened at school. How do I know this? I know this because I go to middle school every day (okay, true, not on Saturday and Sunday). I go to middle school five days a week. (Okay, true, not in the summer.) I go to middle school five days a week, but not in the summer, and I know that every day, there's something hard that happens. Sometimes, it's a big hard thing, like you had a disagreement with your best friend, or you saw someone get bullied, or you were the one who got bullied. Sometimes, it's a tiny hard thing, like having to ask why a bunch of times and feeling clueless, or you got bewildered by a test. Right now, think about the hard thing from today. What was it? Write about it in the incredibly divine, gorgeous blank space in your journal, or on a sheet of paper, or on your bathroom walls (wait, scratch that idea, just use some toilet paper). Here's your title:

The Bad Thing That Happened Today

Okay, great. Well, it's not great that this bad thing happened. But great for writing about it. (This awesome writer and thinker named Henri Nouwen once said that we have to write and talk about the hard stuff that happens to us so we can get through it.[6] That's true.)

Now, make a list of all the things you *don't know* about this bad thing. Try to come up with a list of seven. You can number them in either real, human numbers, or space gnome numbers, which are highly secretive and even flammable.

Now, you might be saying to yourself (or shouting loudly to me so that I can hear you), "How can I list seven things that are below the surface if I don't know what things are below the surface?!"

Thanks for shouting—I heard you loud and clear! (And I even included your excellent question in the book, as you can see in the above paragraph.) And that is *the* question to ask: How can you list seven things below the surface if you can't see below the surface? Well, you *guess*. That's right, take seven wild, crazy, beautiful guesses as to what was going on that you couldn't see.

For example, I remember a time I felt like crying (and, okay, *did* cry) when my six-year-old son (who loves drawing and art) said, "I'm not a good artist." When he said this, I had to stop and take a breath. It was hard for both of us: I was having a hard time understanding why he was having a hard time—he's such a great artist. To see just what the heck was going on under the surface, I had to take a few guesses at things I couldn't yet see. When I did that, my list looked something like this:

1. Maybe one of my son's friends saw a picture he drew and told him that it looked stupid or something.

2. Maybe my son heard ME say that I felt like I wasn't a good writer, or a good teacher, or a good dirt digger, or (please, no!) a good dad. And if that is one of the reasons, then maybe I need to think more about what I say in front of my son when I'm having a bad day!

3. Maybe he thinks good art can ONLY look one way because of the books we're reading. Maybe we need to get some books with pictures by Picasso. Yes! Picasso—who painted people with way too many faces and extra legs and whose bodies were half horse and all kinds of other crazy stuff!

4. Maybe I'm crying because when I was a kid I felt like I wanted to be good at something (basketball? writing? walking on only my big toes?) and felt like I was terrible at it. So maybe what my son is saying now touches all that stuff I felt when I was six years old . . .

You get the idea! (I hope.) I won't bore you with all seven of my things. Making this list of seven things beneath the surface doesn't always mean these seven possibilities are right on the nose, but they do help us to think deeper, to consider what else might be going on, and when we do that, we sometimes find that we have ideas for how to keep going. We get ideas and inspiration for what we can do to make things better. But if we just stay on the surface and stare at each other while the hard stuff happens to us, we might never get to these powerful (and, okay, sometimes painful) places where we realize all kinds of amazing stuff that can help us and people around us grow.

So have at it! Seven things beneath the surface of your hard thing . . .

Awesome! No, not awesome that there are now seven things you don't understand about this bad thing that happened to you. Awesome that you're now coming to understand something important: we can't see it all. None of us can. Not even teachers. Not even parents.

Your seven guesses may not be true. But that really doesn't matter all that much. What matters is that you're starting to see that *life exists below the surface of what we can see.* And when you give yourself permission to wonder about what's happening below the surface, you tend to treat yourself (and others) with more kindness. This fabulously ancient philosopher named Philo is attributed to have said, "Be kind, for everyone you meet is fighting a hard battle." This is true, and it's really a fancy way of saying: everybody has a lot of hard stuff going on below the surface, yourself included.

I have so many of these seven-item lists that if each was worth a dollar, I would be able to easily pay to forge a mission to the planet of the space gnomes to *get back all that garlic bread!* Because there's so much beneath the surface that I do not see in each situation around me, there's so much of the iceberg that still waits to be discovered.

And the cool thing about life is that we're all carrying around tons of these lists of seven things that are below the surface of what happens to us. That means all your friends, teachers, parents, librarians, servers in restaurants, doctors, rocket scientists, janitors, brain surgeons—*everyone ever everywhere*—have many lists like this. We don't always realize it, and we don't always get the chance to reflect and find out what's really going on underneath the events or feelings that we have. But the cool thing is this: we can start to explore the lists for ourselves and realize what's going on beneath the surface in our lives. Yes. And the second also-cool thing is this: we can help other people explore their own lists by asking them questions and then really listening with kindness. We might learn a  heck of a lot about other people, and a lot about ourselves, by getting past the surface.

Be willing to dig a little deeper. Be willing to undercover some other possibilities. Hey, maybe we'll see each other digging. If so, I promise to wave! And if you need a shovel, I have loads!

6

TEACHERS ARE *HOMO* *SAPIENS* TOO

Here's where you see what pencil sharpening, getting yelled at in class, sneezing, and the squishiness of the human heart all have in common. Hint: it's *not* that they are all new rides at Disney World.

A STORY ABOUT A BAD MOVE

I am a middle school teacher because of a heck of a lot of love: for students! for writing! for reading! Huge heaps of huzzahs hovering everywhere! However, this is a true story about a very bad move I made . . . a move *not* out of love.

It was a Friday, last period. It had been a rough class. Everybody was exhausted and ready for the weekend. (Their teacher was feeling the same way this particular day too.) Most students really didn't want to finish the activity we were working on, so there was a whole lot of noise and chatter in the classroom with practically no one doing their work. "Everybody freeze!" I said fiercely to all my students. "It's too loud and crazy in here right now! Stop!"

Of course, my fierce command was itself pretty loud and a little crazy, so I really only added to the general hullabaloo. Everything did go silent, however, as my students weren't used to hearing me roar like that. But right at that very silent moment a boy named Window, quiet, kind Window, got up from his seat and went over to the pencil sharpener. He was the only student in class who had *actually* been working on the activity, and he needed a sharper pencil to *keep* working on the activity.

But I was exasperated. The space gnomes had gotten to me—where was all my garlic bread? Ahhhh! "Did you just hear the direction?!" I snapped at Window in a voice way too loud and fierce.

Well, Window about looked like he was going to cry. And then, of course, I about felt like I was going to cry. But if Window and

I started crying right in the middle of last period on a Friday, well, things were only going to get worse. This was a bad move. I'd made a very, very bad move. And I apologized to Window, and we eventually ended the class. Subsequently, I apologized, and agonized, and apologized again. Window (the kind and considerate soul that he was) forgave me for yelling at him so ridiculously.

So what's the deal? Why was I so mean and so different from what I really believe and *wanted* to be like as a teacher in that moment?

WHAT IS A *HOMO SAPIENS*?

To figure out why I was so mean—so different from what I always desperately wanted to be as a teacher!—we need to figure out what the term *Homo sapiens* means. So I'll give you a moment to check with someone right next to you. Go ahead. If you don't know what a *Homo sapiens* is, tap the person next to you on the shoulder and ask. If it's your dog, ask anyway. Hey, stranger things have happened.

Any luck? If your friend doesn't know, or says something like, "You don't know?!" (which means *your friend* doesn't know either), then here you go: *Homo sapiens* is just a fancy, scientific way of saying *a human being*. It's kind of like the word *parsimonious*, which really just means *cheap*. It's using a long, weird-sounding word (or phrase) to mean a simple one.

And indeed, teachers *are* human beings, just like you. In fact, we're not all that different from you.

In this chapter, I'm going to let you in on a load of secrets. These are the kind of top secrets that could make me a wanted man, or at the very least, could get me in massive amounts of troublesome danger and dangerous trouble. But you're worth it. I want you to succeed in your mission to make life meaningful in middle school, and so I've got to let some secrets about teachers out of the bag. (Don't tell them I told you, but it's all true stuff here.)

Here we go. You ready?

Good.

Secret #1: If teachers are having a crappy day, they might take it out on you.

Before I explain this secret to you, first let me say that anytime a teacher tells you that you're doing something wrong, it doesn't mean the teacher is really having an awful day and you just happen to be an available scapegoat. No, sometimes you really are doing something wrong, and you need to be told, "Hey, stop it!" I've had to say this to students I adore—but it's important to know when you're making a bad decision, to take the reprimand in stride, and to make changes. So this secret isn't about you always being right.

However.

This secret *is* about realizing that if you do something pretty small—maybe you get up to sharpen your pencil like Window did, or you sneeze loudly in class while your teacher is talking, and he flips out on you, giving you three detentions and telling you that your choice to sneeze instead of holding it in was rude, unacceptable, and thoughtlessly inconsiderate—it's probably a fact that your teacher is having a really, really, no-good, miserably crappy day.

Think about how often you feel like the whole world is against you. Maybe you feel this way right now. Maybe this morning, you spilled the milk all over everything as you were trying to pour it into your cereal bowl. Then on the way to the bus stop, you stepped in a huge mud puddle left over from last night's rainstorm. Then at school, you and your best friend got into a fight. Chances are, you're not going to be the friendliest middle schooler in town.

Well, teachers are *exactly* like you. We have days like this too. So maybe your teacher gets really angry at you because you didn't do your homework. She starts saying things like, "Are you ever going to do *any* work this year, Fiddlebutt?" She keeps on talking, making you feel really lousy about yourself and about the entire universe. Well, maybe she was up all night with her one-year-old son while he was coughing and throwing up, and she came to school this morning exhausted and worried sick. Chances are she's taking out some of that worry and anger on you.

Or perhaps your teacher is reaming you out because you were running in the hallways. You know you're not supposed to run in the hallways. It's a school rule, posted everywhere in the building. But you were running late to class because you were constipated in the bathroom and had to wait until some other kids left so you could really push (not wanting to make those pooping sounds while someone else was in there with you). Doesn't matter. You never run in the hallways. Ever. And this teacher could've stopped you, given a stern but calm warning, and let you go on your way. But instead, he's grabbing you and dragging you to the main office, where he says he's going to have the secretary call your mother *immediately*. Well, maybe that teacher is still coping with the death of his own mother. Or maybe he didn't get a promotion he wanted, and he's been angry at the world ever since. Or maybe his favorite contestant on *Dancing with the Stars* was voted off the night before. In any case, maybe he's taking it out on you.

Okay—why am I telling you all of this? Why am I risking a whole bunch of teachers getting really mad at me? Why do you even need to know this stuff? There's one big reason you need to know that teachers are human in this way, and it's this: *it's not always about you.* In middle school, you're going to think that the way people treat you is always about you. If a teacher says you're a terrible writer, you're probably going to believe this person and think you'll never be able to write. If a teacher says you're awful at speaking in public, chances are you're going to believe it and hate public speaking for a long, long, long time. If a teacher reams you out for something small you do, chances are you're going to think you're a pretty lousy human being.

[I keep my ideals, because] in spite of everything I still believe that people are really good at heart.
—Anne Frank, a brave young Jewish girl who was hidden during the Nazi genocide in Germany

But all of this isn't true. Sometimes people say to others what they believe about themselves, and they treat others the way they feel about themselves. Teachers do this too. It's hard to really believe, but it's true. I've known a lot of teachers, and I think I know myself pretty well, too, and all of them at one point or another (including me) have taken out our own frustration, pain, or worry on a student who didn't deserve it. It's not right. It's not fair. But it does happen.

So remember that no teacher has the ability to tell you who you are or how much you're worth. If a teacher yells at you, or makes you feel really lousy, it may not even be about you—and remember, teachers are *Homo sapiens* too, after all.

Secret #2: Teachers are actually students too!

Not many middle school students know that their teachers are being graded. Sound strange? It's true. Think about how you feel when a big test is coming up, how nervous you get, and how even though

you may have studied incredibly hard, you are still afraid that you're going to bomb the test. Well, in just the same way, your teachers have to take tests. The tests are called *observations*. Kind of a strange thing to call a teacher test, I know, but that's what they call it, and you'll see why.

Basically, it goes like this: The principal, or vice principal, or a space gnome secretly disguised as a normal *Homo sapiens* asks your teacher to give him or her lesson plans. Your teacher's lesson plans are kind of like homework. They include all the stuff the teacher will do with you, the goals she or he has for your class, and how your teacher will check to see if these goals are met. Teachers have to write all of this stuff down (which, trust me, can get pretty boring sometimes) and hand it in to the principal or someone else to check it over. Then the principal or vice principal will slide into the back of the classroom one day—like a fox, or like a space gnome who has covered itself in slippery garlic butter—to watch your teacher teach. If your teacher isn't doing a good job, your teacher will get a bad grade. If your teacher gets a lot of bad grades, your teacher might be fired. Teachers don't get fired all that often, but I've seen it happen!

So your teachers are students too. They have to prove that they know what they're doing. And we know that grading is *not* what matters most, but many teachers worry about their grades a lot! Deep down, your teachers want to learn to be better teachers; they want to learn for learning's sake. But adults sometimes struggle with the same stuff you do (as we'll find out in the next chapter).

Secret #3: Teachers are sometimes just as confused as you are.

You know how you sometimes feel like you just don't have the slightest clue about what to do? Maybe, like I did in middle school, you're trying on all these different styles and ways of acting, trying to figure out who the real you is. One day, you act silent and strong, the next you're trying to be funny and the life of the party. One day, you dress like your pants were stitched to ride just below your two butt cheeks, and the next, you're looking suave with a belt and a classy shirt.

A lot of teachers are kind of like that. They're not quite sure how best to teach sometimes. They might try being funny and relaxed one day, but then if they lose control of the classroom, the next day you see them come in really stern and firm and making demands. Or they may just be confused as to what they really want to do with all of you delightful people. I have talked with teachers who, five minutes before they were about to go into a class to teach you, still didn't have a clue as to what they were going to do that day. (I can even remember myself doing that once in a while.)

You just have to learn how to deal with the hand you're dealt. . . . Sometimes, you have to take your hand of cards and make a collage.
—Kathryn Erskine, National Book
Award–winning author and super-kind human being

But when the bell rings and class starts, most of your teachers are going to act the *complete opposite* way. They're going to act like they know everything, and have it all together, and know exactly what to do, and it's your fault if it doesn't all get done. That's not always the truth. A lot of times, teachers are pretty confused and, like most human beings, try to cover up their own confusion by acting like they know the answers.

Teachers don't know everything! (Here's the really crazy news: No one knows everything. Not even the principal. Not even your parents. Not even the president. Everyone gets confused.)

And sometimes what teachers need most—like you—is the chance to start again from the beginning. They need to try something differently, to grow, to learn, and to realize that they, too, are still very much learners!

Secret #4: Teachers sometimes feel like giving up.

You know how you feel when you've been working on some school assignment for a heck of a long time, and instead of learning anything, it feels more like you're banging a frying pan against your head, and you just want to say, "Forget this, home dawg! I give up!"

Teachers get like that too.

Here's a really super-crazy statistic for you: almost 50 percent of all teachers quit their jobs during their first five years of teaching.[7]

Whoa!

If you've noticed that there are always new teachers starting and other teachers leaving from your middle school (or even your elementary school before that), now you know why. Half of all teachers quit their jobs in their first five years of teaching. In other words, they can get really discouraged—just like you can sometimes—and say, "I can't do this, home slice!" (Well, maybe not in those exact words, but something close to it.)

So sometimes teachers need just as much compassion and help as you do. They're learning and growing and struggling, and they definitely don't have all the answers. There's a chance your teachers may not feel like they are doing a great job at teaching you. But they want to! They want to learn to be good teachers. Keeping that in mind can help.

Secret #5: (Most) teachers really do like you.

Okay, this is a big one. It's important. Most of your teachers really do like you. Most of your teachers didn't think when they were young, *I want to be a teacher so I can make my students' lives about as fun as cutting grass one single blade at a time! I want to make kids writhe in pain and fear, and I want to crush their hearts under my feet and squish all the blood out of them while eating gobs of crushed garlic bread and laughing about it!*

Gruesome image, eh? The good news is that very few teachers actually think that way. In fact, none of the teachers I've ever met thought that way. The truth is, most people become teachers because they actually like students like you. It's true! They think, *Hey, kids are pretty cool. And hey, I love math. I would love to hang out with kids and teach them about what I love—math!*

Now, I know what you're probably thinking—*Luke! Trust me, you haven't met MY teacher. He seriously hates students. He hates me—I know it. I saw him reading a book titled* How to Hate Kids and Make Sure They Know You Hate Them. *The other kids in seventh grade all agree with me: he flunks us all just because we use our lockers or talk about soccer. My teacher is crazy mean—you are SO wrong, Luke!*

I hear you, Flibitty-Ibitty. But wait—please, wait! Teachers don't always show their joy for students and learning as much as they should.

Sometimes teachers get overwhelmed—like other humans—and they forget to tell you how much they like you, or how proud of you they are, or how much they love talking about poetry with you. It isn't good that teachers forget this stuff, and it isn't right, but we forget it nonetheless. That's why a lot of times teachers need reminders, just like you. Teachers need people to tell us to make sure that we're having fun with our students and that we're telling our students stuff like, "Hey, Flibitty-Ibitty, I really like teaching you." Just like my student, Window, at the start of this chapter, you might feel like your teachers hate you because of something they've said. But they very often don't! And it's always okay to go up to teachers after class and tell them that you felt demeaned or a little hurt by what they've said. That can actually open up a great conversation and allow the teacher to share some good with you too!

There you have 'em—the five secrets about teachers that no one else has told you and probably won't. They're all true. I swear. They're secrets I've seen in my own life as a teacher and in the lives of all the people that I have taught with at three different schools.

You need to know these secrets about teachers because they'll help you understand that teachers are *Homo sapiens* too. Teachers are still learning new things, just like you, and even though teachers seem like they know it all, they don't. No one does. It's okay not to know it all and to keep learning, and growing, and practicing. After all, the real point of school isn't to get good grades, and it isn't just to learn a bunch of information to memorize and then repeat.

No.

That would be a total waste of everyone's time.

Instead, the point of school is to learn how to use your voice to share your ideas, to solve problems, and to work with other *Homo sapiens* to grow and encourage and challenge one another. That's it. That's the whole deal.

People are going to try to convince you that school is about a lot of other things. But it's not. It's about growing into the person you are supposed to be and working with others to grow and solve some problems—in math and English, sure, but also in life.

Especially in life.

And teachers, like all human beings, sometimes forget what really matters. When *you* learn and grow and ask questions and get excited and explore, you remind us teachers about what really matters. You remind us that, *Hey, we like you!* And you remind us why we wanted to teach in the first place.

EXERCISE
Digging Deeper with Your Teacher

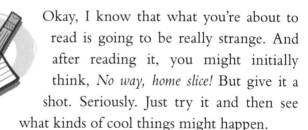 Okay, I know that what you're about to read is going to be really strange. And after reading it, you might initially think, *No way, home slice!* But give it a shot. Seriously. Just try it and then see what kinds of cool things might happen.

In your journal (or super-cool gadget), try this: write down the questions you would love to ask your teachers. These could be questions that are super serious, like:

"When did you first know that you wanted to become a teacher?" Or these could be questions that are super silly, like: "If you had to choose between eating only peanut butter M&M's for the rest of your life *or* having to put pretzel sticks in your ears every morning and leaving them there for the whole day, which would you choose?" Write down ten questions like this.

Then once you've got your list, tuck it into your binder or your backpack or the back pocket of your favorite pair of jeans that you're going to wear to school the next day. In a moment before class starts, or right after class finishes, or when the bell rings for the end of the day, try asking one of your teachers one of these questions.

Then the next day, you could ask another question of the same teacher, or ask another teacher the same question.

Then the next day—you got it—keep going. When you ask these questions of your teacher, you're going to get to know her or him in a different kind of way. You'll be getting to know the real person underneath that teacher who may have given you a grade you weren't all that thrilled about or who may have gotten angry about sharpening a pencil. (Window, if you happen to be reading this now, *hello again!* And, I am so, so, terribly, completely sorry about that pencil sharpening incident.)

Plus, when you ask your teachers some of these questions, you're also doing something pretty dang awesome for *them.* You're kind of saying to them, "Yeah, yeah, yeah. See? I know that you're a *Homo sapiens.* I know that you're not some psycho teacher-bot cyborg who is programmed by the space gnomes to act a certain way and be unfair, or grade too harshly, or. . ." And when you ask your teachers questions like this, you kind of give your teachers permission to be human too. You might wake something up inside them! And they might even ask you questions in return. And then!

And *then!*

And then, all of a sudden, there are these real, live human beings asking questions of each other and listening to the answers, and wow, that's just pretty cool. (And it might make middle school—and surviving it—even more fun and meaningful.)

One quick warning, though: while your teacher is leading a class and introducing, say, how to find the area of a right triangle, or what a topic sentence is, or how a seed germinates, don't raise your hand and ask, "Mr. Gloober-booster, what's your favorite color?" Because, well, that won't really help matters much! Well-timed curiosity is everything.

So have at it! Create your list of ten questions you'd love to ask your teachers. Here goes!

REMEMBER: EVERYONE IS HUMAN

No matter what kinds of teachers you get (or have now) in middle school, keep these five secrets in mind (and these ten questions!) when you notice something strange. If your math teacher comes in looking super nervous, sweating profusely, maybe she's getting tested by the principal later on that day. If your history teacher is screaming at you for being one millisecond late to class—the same as yesterday, when he *didn't* scream—then maybe he had a really awful argument with his girlfriend the night before.

Keeping these five secrets in mind will help you remember that it's not always about you and that your teachers—though they don't ever tell you this—are, indeed, human.

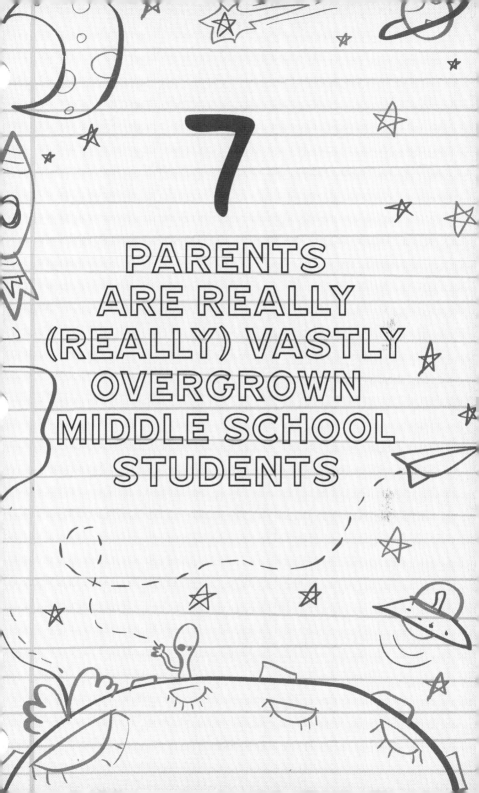

7

PARENTS ARE REALLY (REALLY) VASTLY OVERGROWN MIDDLE SCHOOL STUDENTS

ere's where you see what writing letters, grades, sports expec-tations, and tumultuous nerve car crashes all have in common. Hint: it's *not* that each of these things can be tickled and then cov-ered in melted chocolate.

A STORY ABOUT A PERFECT GRADE

I once had a student named Rocksalt who had to get perfect A+ grades on all of her assignments and in every class for her report card. If she didn't get straight A+ grades, she would act as though the entire world were crumbling at her very feet. Once, I gave Rocksalt a score of 94 on a long essay that she wrote for my class. I thought the essay was excellent—hence the grade of an A—but there were a few areas that could have been stronger.

Well, when I handed Rocksalt back her paper with my com-ments and her grade, she started bawling. You would've thought I had written something like: *You are such an awful writer and a terrible human being on top of it!* Instead, I had given her tons of praise, commented on how clear her essay was, and then gave her a few suggestions to strengthen it even more. But, to add injury to insult, Rocksalt glanced over at her buddy's paper—which had received a 96—and this made the flipping-out-bawling-weeping-world-crumbling experience that much more intense: "You gave *her* a 96? What did she write that I didn't? How *could* you?!" I was flummoxed.

But it all made sense when Rocksalt's mom showed up for parent-teacher conference night. Her mom was the exact same way. Her mom was frustrated with her daughter's grade of a strong A and wondered what she could do the next time to ensure that her daugh-ter could receive a score of 100 on her essay. I'm all for working hard and giving it your absolute best shot, but remember what I said about grades in the first chapter? They're not for comparing, and they're *never* what it's all about!

I looked back at this mother and tried to explain how *proud* of her daughter I was for working so diligently and for earning a 94 on a tough essay assignment. But while I talked of my own happiness regarding her daughter's work, the mother started looking away from me, as if to say, "Yada, yada, yada . . . Give it a rest, will you, buddy? Just tell me how my daughter can get a 100, okay?"

It became painfully clear that Rocksalt's mom wasn't about to get the message. And sadly, I'm sure she went home from that parent-teacher conference and told her daughter that she needed to work harder in English so she could get a perfect 100 on the next essay. (Just because I felt so bad for Rocksalt for having to deal with a parent that demands perfection, I almost gave her a 100 just to see if her mother would then, finally, say she was proud of her daughter. I didn't do it, but I came close!)

Every child is an artist. The problem is how to remain an artist once he grows up.
—Pablo Picasso, painter whose works were originally thought ridiculous by the elite critics

The good news about this story—and Rocksalt—is that she ended up opening her mind a little further than the superficial expectations that had been set for her. By the end of our year together, she had started to see that grades were most certainly *not* what it's all about, and she even started believing me when I told her I was proud of the work she had done—even if it didn't receive a grade of 100. Yes! Rocksalt started to realize that her mom might still be stuck in middle school when it came to grades, but she herself could learn how to get past that way of thinking. And she saw that making life meaningful in middle school is about *way* more than grades.

PARENTAL NERVE CAR CRASHES!

Sometimes it helps to realize that your parents might still be stuck in middle school. Does your dad or mom badger you like crazy and constantly demand that you be a piano prodigy, work harder at soccer, or do extra math problems relentlessly, until your ears grow red, fall off, and scurry around like two tiny mice? If so, it may be because that's what *your parents* wanted when they were in middle school (or high school), and they're kind of still stuck there. Even though they graduated and moved on, maybe part of their brains are still trapped in the past.

Some of the stuff you're reading about in this book, and (hopefully!) trying to put into practice, may actually have never been learned by your parents. Your parents may be constantly comparing themselves to everyone around them and feeling crappy about who they are. Maybe they haven't yet learned that comparison is the thief of joy, as you have (word up, home slice!). They might *still* be thinking that space gnomes are kind of cute, bald little creatures who just like buzzing around and, well, if they steal some garlic bread every now and then, is that so bad? After all, don't space gnomes get a little hungry sometimes too?

Or maybe they haven't learned that love is really about being whole on your own and encouraging another human being. Maybe they're still caught in the trap of thinking they'll only be loved if they look a certain way or act a certain way or talk a certain way. That could explain a lot if your parents are fighting the way mine did when I was a kid.

Or maybe they never learned that people are like icebergs—much of a person is below the surface. So they keep looking around and thinking that everyone else has got it made. They think they're the only parents who can't figure out what's right, or what to do, or how to relate to other people. Icebergs are the key! (As you already know so well.)

So your parents may still be stuck, in some ways, in middle school themselves. It's helpful to keep this in mind when they really get on your nerves, or when you really get on their nerves, or when everybody's nerves get on everybody else's nerves, and soon there's a massive nerve car crash where nerves are piling up right and left, and then the cops show up.

Nerve car crashes happen. The point is this: making your life meaningful in middle school is a lot like making your life meaningful in, well, *life*. The lessons don't necessarily change all that much. In the midst of all the fighting or confusion, remind yourself that your parents are making their way through life with the same kinds of struggles that you're making your way through middle school with—just because they're bigger and hairier doesn't change this fact.

> **It is not the place we occupy which is important, but the direction in which we move.**
> —Oliver Wendell Holmes Sr., Boston-based poet, speaker, and philosopher

Remembering that your parents are, in some ways, overgrown middle school students can help you have a little more patience toward them when the going gets rough.

WHAT *IS* TRUE ABOUT *YOU*

I wish I could end this chapter here. After all, remembering that your parents are sometimes overgrown middle school students is a good ending (I think) and a nice reminder that can really help. However, there are times when thinking of your parents as overgrown middle school students isn't all there is to the equation. No. There are times when we need to recognize if something much, much worse is happening. And much more serious.

First, you need to know that no matter what you say or what you do (ever), you never, ever, ever deserve to be hit. Nothing you could ever say or do deserves a physical response from your parents.

Period. If a parent is hitting you, he or she is not a vastly overgrown middle school student; he or she is an adult who is wrong, and who needs confrontation from someone other than you, namely another adult. Even though the last thing you want to do is talk about this with someone, asking your guidance counselor or a teacher you trust at school is exactly what you need to do. There might be some voice inside of you saying something like, *It was just once . . . it's no big deal,* or *Well, I kind of deserved to be hit. I was swearing and everything.* That voice is wrong. That voice is lying. If one or both of your parents or guardians has hit you, that is abuse. You need to tell someone you can trust at school, and they'll work through a way to help you *and* help your parents.

The second thing you need to hear is that if your parents are telling you that you're good for nothing, or that you're a moron, or that you'll never go to college or do anything worthwhile in life, *they're lying.* It's not true. You are not an idiot. You are not worthless. You *can* go to college if that's something you decide that you want to do. Parents who speak this kind of trash to their children are really admitting the way they feel about themselves—they're saying that *they* feel like trash. But *you* are not trash. No matter how forcefully they may yell these things at you, they're still lying, and they're never right.

I have sat across from parents who've told me that their kid wasn't smart, or couldn't learn, or was stupid or dense or lost. Maybe you need to hear the same thing I told my students when their parents treated them like this: you are smart; you can work hard; you can accomplish a lot in this life; you *are* a worthwhile person.

Demeaning words—whether spoken to you by parents or teachers or anyone else—are words that try to kill your heart. Don't let them do it. Refuse to believe these words, and remind yourself that you *are* a worthwhile person. No one else gets to decide who you are—remember that. Not even your parents.

Students who have been abused often don't want to talk about it. They don't want to bring it up to a teacher or a guidance counselor because they think doing this will only make things worse. And maybe, at first, it might make things worse. But the truth is that keeping abuse or ridicule hidden never makes it better. Bringing it out into the open is hard to do, but it ends up making things better in the long run. A lot better.

So.

Whew.

We talked about some pretty intense stuff in this chapter. Before we head into the Land of Why in the next chapter, try something.

It's scary.

It's dangerous.

It's crazy.

Sound good?

EXERCISE
Getting Real with Mom and Dad

Right now, in some miraculous blank space in your journal, or on a spacious blank page, write a short letter to your mom or dad or both of them. Be really, really honest with them about who you are and about what you hope they see when they look at you. Before you write, try going back

to the super-fabulous writing and drawing you've already done throughout the earlier chapters of this book. What have you learned about yourself? How do you see the world? What are the things you struggle with? What are your hopes? What questions have you asked your teachers that you might also want to ask your parents? You can use some of these really cool insights and ideas to help you craft this letter to your parents.

I told you before, it's crazy. But looking back at all of these other cool things that you've written and thought about will help you realize two things: You've already done some crazy-cool thinking! *And* you already have some things you can share. So here goes! Here's your title:

An Honest Letter to My Mom or Dad

Okay, now are you ready for something even crazier?

Read your mom or dad, or both of them, this letter. Or give it to them. Let them hear who you really are, what you really want them to see when they look at you. After all, it can be pretty hard for a mom or a dad to know exactly what to say to you if you don't give them a little bit of help. And maybe you can help them understand something about who you are that they might be missing.

8

WHY ASK WHY?

Here's where you see what ancient philosophers, golf balls, poetry, and dancing all have in common. Hint: it's *not* that they can also be used as deodorant.

A STORY ABOUT PLATO AND POETRY

Each year in my seventh-grade English class, we read this pretty amazing piece of writing by Plato called *Allegory of the Cave*.[8] Basically, it's a story that this ancient, incredibly wise guy named Socrates told, and Plato (one of his followers) wrote down. It goes like this.

Socrates said to imagine that someone was born inside of a cave, and all that person ever saw or knew was the darkness of that cave. But it gets crazier. Socrates then said to imagine that the whole time this person was growing up in the cave, there was this crazy shadow puppet show happening on the back wall of the cave. Shadows! All right!

Anyway, Socrates said that if a baby grew up into a not-baby just seeing only shadows of people and other puppet things—never leaving the cave the whole time to see anything in the real world— then he or she might actually think that these shadows were *real things and real people.*

Then Socrates gets really freaky. He says that if you or I or someone who didn't live in the cave brought this person up into the light, showed the cave dweller real things and real people, and told this person that all those shadows back on

the cave wall were fake—not the real thing—then the person who had lived his or her whole life in the cave wouldn't believe us and instead tell us that what we're saying is totally wacky, and that we were wacky!

The point of the cave allegory for Socrates was that if we accept something long enough, we kind of just assume that—of course!—it's true, and we don't question it. Then when people try to get us to question our assumption, we tell them that they are the crazy ones!

Once a guy asked Socrates what he'd prefer to think about life: "I prefer nothing," said Socrates, "unless it is true." Socrates believed that if something wasn't true, it wouldn't be meaningful. And the only way to find out what is meaningful, he said, is to ask *loads* of questions.

Okay, so why did we go and talk about Socrates and Plato and some smelly ancient cave? (Hey, I never said the cave was smelly! Did you add that part in?)

Good question. You're already asking why, and that's good.

I told you about Plato and the cave because of a student named Caveman that I had once. Caveman loved basketball. Everything was basketball. He ate basketballs for breakfast; he ate basketballs for lunch; he ate garlic bread for dinner (even basketballs need a break, right?). He played basketball every chance he got, and to him, basketball was all that mattered in life. Basketball was awesome.

Poetry was *not*. Poetry really stunk.

But when Caveman was in my class, we read (and wrote) *a lot* of poetry. We read a poem in every single class—which makes 180 poems that year! And after two weeks of this, Caveman said, pretty clearly, "Poetry really stinks, Mr. Reynolds."

"Why?" I asked Caveman.

"Because it's bad," he replied.

"Why?" I asked Caveman.

"Because it's boring," he replied.

"Why?" I asked Caveman.

"Because *it just stinks*," Caveman replied.

Well, this conversation continued for approximately seven and a half hours. But after those seven and a half hours, Caveman noticed that some of the poetry we read in class was actually from hip-hop songs, from rock songs, from four-year-olds saying the most hilarious things, from gravestones, from all over the place.

Once we'd read all these other kinds of poetry, Caveman asked, "Why didn't I ever know that this stuff was poetry too?"

"Exactly!" I replied.

"Why?" Caveman asked.

"Exactly!" I replied.

And then, *this* conversation continued for approximately seven and a half hours. But this conversation was a heck of a lot more fun, because Caveman was asking why, and he was thinking, and he was seeing poetry, and the classroom, and maybe even himself, a little bit differently.

WHY ASK WHY?

Some people hate the question: Why?

I love it. I love it so much that if it were on the dance floor alone, and everyone was looking at Why—saying stuff like, "Hey, look at that loser, all alone with no one to dance with! Ha! Ha! Ha!"—then I would saunter over to Why and say, in my most seductive whisper that only I can muster, "Wanna dance?" That's how much I love Why.

Why?

I'm glad you asked. I am thrilled that you asked. The kind of thrilling sensation that is running all over me now—from you asking why I love Why—makes me want to dance. If you were here with me, I would, in fact, teach you how to swing dance. And then we would swing dance to some really hip, upbeat swing song (as you would do if you were a student in my English class, and we had just finished watching the film *Swing Kids* after studying World War II).

Since you're not here, and I would feel pretty silly swing dancing around my living room alone, I'll forego the dancing part and instead tell you why I love Why so much.

Whoops. Sorry. I did just do one little swing routine, mainly a few steps and then a spin move when I spun you around in my imagination. You probably don't feel dizzy or anything, but in case you do—in your imagination—take a moment before proceeding to the next paragraph. Breathe deeply. In through your nose, out through your mouth. Or is it in through your mouth, out through your nose? Try both. But

deeply, and peacefully, as if you are a butterfly floating on a rose-bush, then running away from a wild tiger who is trying to eat you for a snack. No, no, no . . . I mean, as if you are a butterfly, period.

Okay, here's why I love Why so much: it's the answer to all of life.

I know what you're probably thinking: *Luke, what in the heck, man! How can a question be the answer to all of life? Dude, man, you're like, so wacked. I'm seriously finished with your strange book. Word. I'm gonna get out of here and go hang with my friends at Mickey D's.*

No!

Come back!

Let me explain. *Why* is the answer to all of life because it's the question that, above all else, unlocks meaning in every book, experience, movie, look, and everything else. When we ask why about something, it's like a firework goes off inside of our heads and our entire brains light up like the Fourth of July. Our brains can see . . . *everything!* (Even though our brains don't have any eyes, you know what I mean, right?) Remember how many amazing neurons we have—and all those remarkable connections they make?!

I think, at a child's birth, if a mother could ask a fairy godmother to endow it with the most useful gift, that gift would be curiosity.
—Eleanor Roosevelt, women's rights' activist and powerful speaker and writer

Case in point #1: For English class, you have to read a book about a boy who hates his father. Throughout the entire book, this boy is talking on and on about what a jerk his father is and how much he hates him. You read the whole book, and at the end of it, there's this really sad scene where the dad and the son are hugging and crying on each other's shoulders and, if this were a movie, there'd be some seriously sad but kind-of-hopeful music playing in the background. So you close the cover of the book, and you ask, "Why did the dad and son finally hug?"

Yes! Bingo! (And, if you had read that book in my class and asked that question, I would have lifted you out of your seat and placed you on my shoulders and carried you around the classroom while I belted out the song "We Are the Champions" by Queen.)

Case in point #2: You're going out with this guy who is pretty suave. I mean, this guy's *hair* is so hot it just spontaneously combusts into flame. And things are going well. He says he likes you a lot. But he wants to kiss you. He really wants to kiss you. *Hmmm,* you think, *Why does he want to kiss me so badly? Why can't we just talk, like we normally do?*

Yes (again)! Bingo (again)!

Case in point #3: Your teacher is talking about this new project you're going to start, where you have to count lots of different-colored golf balls. Then you have to put the golf balls in different spots all over this big chart that you'll have to make. The more your teacher talks, the less you understand why you're doing this project. While your head is starting to feel like little elves are doing some sort of chorus-line dance up there, a question forms: Why? So you raise your hand and ask, "Why are we using golf balls for this? Why are we using this chart?"

Yes! Yes! Yes! Bingo! Bingo! Bingo! (Man, if you only knew how badly I want to swing dance right now.)

123

In all three of these cases, asking why is the answer in itself. See, asking why proves that your brain is actually present, awake, and turned on. Those neurons are connecting with other neurons in a seriously boisterous neuron fiesta! People who ask why are people who are thinking about what they're experiencing, and those kinds of people are freaking awesome. They're awesome because they are keeping the connections their neurons make *alive* instead of letting those connections slowly die.

Letting those beautiful neuron connections in your gooey brain die looks like this: You're going through your life and certain things confuse you, but you just keep going without asking why. Certain things don't make sense, but you say, "Whatever," just to get the grade, or get that first kiss out of the way, or wear the brand name, and keep on going. Certain things make you really, really, super curious, but you don't pursue them and say, "Oh well," and tell your curiosity to shut up. You do stuff just enough to trick your mind into *thinking* that you're actually learning, but your brain's connections aren't staying alive. You may get some good grades by going through the motions. You may get a super-cool boy or girl to go out with you by going through the motions. You may even make the sports team by going through the motions. But all of these things won't be as meaningful as they could be, because you won't really know *why* you're doing what you're doing.

And if you let all of this stuff pass you by *without* asking why, you'll be doing exactly what the space gnomes want you to do! *Not* asking why is kind of like pulling out a freshly baked loaf of garlic bread from the oven, taking a deep whiff of the garlicky goodness, and then handing it out the window to a floating space gnome who happens to be waiting right there. Instead of enjoying the taste and the joy and the full depth of that garlic bread, you're just kind of baking it and then passing it off, letting all the goodness be stolen from you. No!

Life is either a daring adventure or nothing at all.
—Helen Keller, deaf and blind activist who dramatically changed education and people's perceptions

It *is* harder to learn in a way that keeps all the beautiful connections in your brain alive than to just let them die. I'll be honest about that. Fully alive learning is when you ask why about all kinds of stuff. In doing so, you may annoy a lot of people. You may even annoy yourself when you ask why a lot. But you're really learning. You might try new things. Or you may even still decide to do a lot of the same stuff, but you'll have a reason behind it. You'll have some real thoughts behind why you're doing what you're doing.

Just like Caveman, you'll start to see stuff around you in a new way, and you'll wonder why you never saw life like that before. And as you wonder about this, you'll have pretty cool conversations that might last seven and a half hours, and then you might even write some poetry afterward!

EXERCISE
A Crazy Collection of Questions

Now, do you have a clock or stopwatch nearby? Or a clock-stopwatch on your cell phone? *You have a cell phone?! Seriously?* I didn't get a cell phone until I was twenty-four! (Okay, they weren't invented until I was seventeen, but still!)

Okay, find some awesome blank space in your journal or on a piece of paper, and time yourself. For three minutes, write every why question you can think of. No matter what it is, just write it down. Ready?

Go!

Three Minutes of Why

Yes!

Now go through your list (or bubble, or cloud, or mountain, or space gnome—shaped blob of questions) and just read them all. Just let your gooey brain take in all the beauty—all the curiosity and wonder—that is inside it. Being brilliant means you are curious about a lot of things, and you *wonder* a lot. That's it. So keep asking, "Why?" Keep wondering. Every time you do, you're becoming even more brilliant.

9

ARE GRADES FOR EATING?

ere's where you see what chicken pot pie, hard work, *all* the letters of the alphabet, and soul have in common. Hint: it's *not* that they will cure moon-crater-sized pimples.

A STORY ABOUT SOUL

A long, long time ago, in a galaxy far from here—I mean, in a town not too far from where I am currently a teacher, I did something called student teaching. What this means is that I hung out in a real teacher's classroom while I was learning to be a teacher.

The teacher who I got to hang out with was a pretty amazing guy. He had an incredibly long mustache, and he smiled a lot and told great stories about amazing writers. So I was pretty happy. One day, he was teaching me how to write comments for students on an essay and how to grade that essay. Passing me a student's essay, he said, "What do you think?"

I read it twice and looked at the rubric that the teacher gave me beforehand (which is like a big grading sheet with all those boxes and grids that we teachers sometimes give you with your work). Then I said, "Well, it does everything on the rubric, so I'm thinking it gets an A."

"You got it!" the teacher replied. I smiled. I was right! But then the teacher added, "The thing is, Luke, *that essay has no soul.*"

Now, if you're wondering, *Luke, how the heck would an essay even have a soul in the first place?!* then you are not alone. That was the exact same thing I wondered. And wondering about that made me really want to eat some garlic bread. Or a very large chicken pot pie. Since we had neither in the classroom, though, we talked instead.

The student who wrote the essay had answered everything right—she had found all the right evidence and made a strong case for her argument. But there was no life in the essay—no real connection to the novel or herself, or to others, or to growth, or, well, to anything other than the rubric. Even though she had done amazing by the rubric's standards, this student writer had missed something. Because getting a perfect score on the rubric doesn't always mean that you become more alive or that you feel deep-down amazing.

WHAT WE CAN (AND CAN'T) EAT

By now, you know that I love a big loaf of garlic bread. And I mean, I love the *whole* loaf. Ask anyone you know who may possibly know me, and they'll tell you that it's true. I can eat an entire loaf of garlic bread all by myself.

129

I also love mangoes. Man, can I put down some mangoes! I once ate seven consecutive mangoes, only stopping to use the bathroom once, between mango number four and mango number five.

I even love chicken pot pie. Think about it: gravy goodness, tender chicken, a few vegetables thrown in there for good measure, and *all of that inside a pie crust.*

Pie crust!

I could probably eat two, maybe three chicken pot pies all on my own (that is, over the course of a day).

Why am I telling you that I enjoy eating all of these foods? First of all: Don't you too? Well, your favorites may not be exactly the foods I mentioned, but I want you to think about a food you love so much that you could eat gobs and gobs of it until you're wondering, *Why in the heck didn't anyone stop me from eating five servings of garlic-flavored macaroni and cheese?!*

Second, the reason I'm telling you this is because these items are delicious. We can insert said foods into our mouths, chew, swallow, and *voilà,* a meal!

But we can't eat grades. I mean, we really *cannot* eat grades. I once had a student who tried, and the result wasn't pleasant. I'll call her Leanna-Fe-Fi-Fo-Fanna to avoid any embarrassment for my real student (whose name was actually Leanna Hemoglobin). See, where I was teaching middle school at the time, in Massachusetts, all of us teachers passed out report cards to our students at the very end of the last Friday of the term. If your school is anything like mine, well, students swarm around the homeroom teachers, waiting like vultures to see how they've performed. How had we teachers graded *their* achievement?

Of course, part of the motivation for this swarming business is that your parents, many of them, often promise to buy you things like

Nintendo-Xbox-iPod-uPod-We-All-Pod-Super-Systems and other such technologically advanced devices. *If* you did well enough, that is.

Well, I am sorry to report, Leanna-Fe-Fi-Fo-Fanna did *not* do well enough. In fact, she did so poorly that she crumpled up her entire report card on the spot in my class, Room 33, and then proceeded to stuff it into her mouth. But Leanna-Fe-Fi-Fo-Fanna forgot a very, extremely important truth: *You can't eat grades.*

When surviving middle school, it's super important to remember this non-eating-capacity of grades. No matter what, grades just can't be grilled and gobbled. Even *if* you work hard and do the homework the teacher assigns (which you might think is so incredibly crappy that you sometimes wonder if it's actual crap masquerading as a work-

sheet), *and* you follow the rules the teachers and principal and vice principal and secretaries and hallway monitors and janitors and school pets set up for you to follow (even if they are so incredibly illogical as to make you think, *Did a human being actually think up this rule?*), and you stay focused in school (even if your teacher is asking you to focus on tennis balls, or a big black hole, or a marshmallow that your teacher keeps claiming is some kind of nucleus or electron or nucleo-electrolytosis proton)—well, even *if* you do all these things and get the gold medal of a good grade, it isn't going to fill you up in a deep-down kind of way.

No matter how badly you want to get straight As, or make the honor roll, or the high honor roll, or the I'm-so-smart-even-Einstein-would-have-trembled-at-the-feet-of-my-gigantic-brain roll, you still can't eat grades.

Grades are never going to fill you up like food.

Grades will never give you that feeling of pure satisfaction that you get after you drink a cup of hot chocolate and eat some cookies after playing King of the Hill outside in the snow all day because school was canceled due to the storm.

Grades will never settle in your stomach, stretch themselves out in your belly, and relax you like that special dish only your dad or mom can make.

Grades are never going to fill you up.

It will feel good when you earn an A. It will feel even better when you earn two As. It may even feel like you're the master of the universe when you earn three or four or five or six or seven or eight or nine As. (How many classes do you have to take at your middle school?! Jeez!)

But that good feeling won't ever fill you up completely. It will show you that you've worked hard—yes—and that's a great thing. But because grades are based on your actions—based on what you actually do and then how someone judges you for it—grades won't ever be able to give you peace of mind in the way that a delicious meal gives you peace of belly. Your report card is always going to be based on how someone judges you. Your grades are always going to be someone else's measurement of your abilities, work, and ideas. In this way, grades are never going to help you find peace, because they will always be completely out of your deep sense of self.

I can recall getting a C− on an essay I wrote because a college professor said it was too personal, and then having a magazine publish a similar essay because the editor said it *was* so personal! And I've gotten an A+ on a short story that no one, anywhere, ever, has agreed to put in a magazine. The grade itself can't ever measure the true worth of something—and if we look to the grade for the deep sense of peace, we might find ourselves being thrown wildly all around.

It's good to work hard in middle school. It's fine and natural to want to get good grades for the hard work that you do. But if you're doing it *only* because of the grades, or if you're doing it only because your mom promised she would buy you those $595 pair of Abercrombie and Fitch underpants, well, something is wrong.

The space gnomes want you to believe that the grades are what it's all about in middle school. If you get that big, beautiful A, then

you really have made it—and if you haven't, then you're totally lost! The space gnomes want you to be so focused on getting an A that you forget all about the garlic bread baking in the oven, and they can swoop in and snatch it up!

But while grades aren't what it's all about, you've still got to work hard in middle school. *Really hard.* I made my students write more than they ever thought they could. (And if you were my student, and I was teaching you right now, I would make you write a whole heaping pile of words. Then I would make you read them, and think about them, and talk with me about them. Then I would make you write a whole new heaping pile of words. Then, together we'd pour some pasta sauce on both heaping piles and eat them, along with some tasty garlic bread on the side. Wait, scratch that: words are like grades—you can't eat them, either.)

But don't let the grades become the rewards for the hard work. The truth is this (and it's a little confusing): the hard work is the reward for the hard work.

It is good to have an end to journey toward; but it is the journey that matters, in the end.
—Ursula K. Le Guin, bestselling author of fantasy novels, who also has one of the coolest names ever

If you're thinking: *What, the hard work is the reward?! That's an error. Don't publishing companies, like, have anyone to edit these books so that there aren't stupid mistakes like this in them? I mean, for real!*

That wasn't a mistake. What I mean is this: the hard work that you do on your homework, projects, essays, collages, pictograms, pictographs, picto-pictos, and other assignments *is the reward itself.* Because, while you can't eat grades, there is something that feels even better than a stomach full of food. And that's looking at something you've created, and being able to say to yourself, "Wow, that's pretty sweet."

No letter that any teacher gives you can ever match your feeling of pride when you know that the work you did is amazing. Most people don't realize that until they're in high school or even college. (And some people don't ever realize it.)

If you can realize now, while you're in middle school, that the grades aren't the point, then you're well on your way to making your life meaningful in middle school. And you're well on your way to doing something meaningful in your life for a purpose other than those five letters of the alphabet. (By the way, there are twenty-one *more* letters in the alphabet—why not spend some time thinking about those ones too?!)

ON THE OTHER HAND . . .

Before I let you stop reading this chapter (if you are, in fact, reading this chapter . . . *are* you reading this chapter? Be honest with me, come on, now . . . *are you?*), I would like to tell you one more thing. The space gnomes *almost* stole this last part of the chapter along with a loaf of garlic bread I was baking, but I managed to snatch both back just in the nick of time.

If you're on the opposite end of the spectrum, and you never did well in school because you haven't done any work and instead prefer to hang out at the local Mickey D's ordering yogurt parfaits and looking cool holding your skateboard, then:

Leave Mickey D's now; go home; do some work.

Not just for the grades—though it would be kind of cool to see an A or a B where there are usually Ds and Fs, right?—but because, as I wrote before, you're going to feel a heck of a lot better doing some work rather than trying to look cool not doing work.

Anyone can do that.

(Okay, fine. I'm not the best at looking cool while not doing any work. But it isn't because I haven't tried. I once spent a full day trying to look super cool while not doing any work, but strangers just kept coming up to me asking things like, "Are you okay?" and "Do you need me to call anyone for you?")

So why not do something that takes a little effort and skill and see how it feels?

All you have to do is write one true sentence. Write the truest sentence that you know.
—Ernest Hemingway, Nobel-Prize winning author
who did 39 rewrites of a novel's ending

EXERCISE
One True Sentence

Right now, take a deep breath. Deeper. Deeper. Yes! And remember that no grade defines who you are. Hard work *for* something is awesome not because of what someone else thinks or how you are judged or measured, but because of what *you* think—first and foremost. Right now, write a single sentence.

Write: I am proud of myself because I work hard.
Write it ten times. Write it a million times. (Okay, maybe not a million. That's a lot of blank space to fill.)

Now, if you *really* want to get crazy, say that sentence out loud. Say it when you're working and you get to a really, really tough essay that even Ernest Hemingway couldn't write. (Remember how I mentioned back in chapter 2 that Ernest Hemingway had to rewrite his novels a bunch before he was happy with them?) Then, keep at that problem— not to get a perfect score, but because working hard makes you stronger, wiser, and feel good deep inside.

10
STUFF

Here's where you see what sleep, hugs, tiny mailmen caught on doorway flowerpots, and kindness all have in common. Hint: it's *not* that you can mix all of these things together in a massive bowl and make chocolate chip pancakes with them.

WHY ANOTHER CHAPTER AND WHY *STUFF*?

Within this book, I've tried to give you the secrets to making middle school meaningful that you might not hear from anyone else. I wanted to take you behind the scenes of your teachers' lives; I wanted to give you a glimpse of your parents that you might not see; I wanted to talk with you straight up about things like love, your brain, keeping your voice strong, becoming the person only you can become, and grades. (And garlic bread. And space gnomes.)

But this chapter is about all the other *stuff*. There's always other stuff, right? Think about anything in your life: there's always one main story—the big picture—but then there are so many important connections! Say you go to your best friend's birthday party and the big story of the night is that one of your friend's parents isn't living at home with the family anymore. It's a huge story (and a sad one too). But that same night, you start thinking about your own parents, and you wonder how your relationship is with them. That's the other stuff. So let's dig into a whole lot of other stuff that this book hasn't dug into yet. Got your shovel ready? Okay, into the soil we go in search of the detail-oriented (but still super-important) stuff!

FIRST ITEM OF STUFF: TAKE INITIATIVE

Initiative is a tough word. I've seen students spell it *initative*, *inatative*, *initititi*, and *inishative*, among other ways. It's a hard word to spell and an even harder word to live. All it really means is that you do something rather than waiting for someone to tell you what to do all the time. It could be that you ask a question, that you get some supplies, that you complete a project, or that you tell people they played a great game, look nice, or are kind human beings— whatever you do, you do it without someone else prompting you to do it.

I once had a student who decided to write a novel. He was only in the seventh grade, but he started staying after school with me twice a week and wrote for an hour each time. He said he wanted to write a book, and it wasn't because someone else told him he needed to write a book. He had initiative, and he decided to go for it. (During the process, he was like caked dirt for those two hours a week after school—no matter what, he wouldn't quit.) By the end of the school year, in June, he had finished his novel. A whole book, and he was only in seventh grade!

Taking initiative means you do something good in your life and in the world, and not just as a reaction. You might pick up some garbage on the hallway floor (whoa!), you might say hi to the janitor, or you might start dressing more *you* and less *them*. Whatever you choose, taking initiative helps you to start becoming a confident middle school student rather than one who's always looking around for someone else to tell you what to do.

SECOND ITEM OF STUFF: LAUGH

To outsmart the space gnomes—who, remember, are trying *very hard* to steal every last crumb of your garlic bread—you have got to laugh in middle school. And when I write the word *laugh*, what I really mean is this: Imagine that a very tiny mailman has just come to your door. This mailman is, oh, say, about nine inches tall. He manages to ring your doorbell because he can jump higher than an NBA basketball player. But on his way back to the ground—*aaaaahhh!*—the tiny mailman has gotten stuck in the rosebush flowerpot by your door because he jumped so high just to reach *your* doorbell to deliver a very tiny package. (Did I not mention the very tiny package?)

So you finally open the door, and you find the tiny mailman helplessly caught in a treacherous tangle of rosebush thorns inside the flowerpot by your door still holding a tiny package. Like any normal person would, you say hello.

"Hello, Tiny Mailman," you say.

"Hello, Tall Seventh Grader," he says.

Then you look at each other for a long, long time.

"Do you need help to get out of those rosebush thorns?" you finally ask.

"Yes," he responds.

So (of course) you go inside and get your dad's nose hair clippers to cut off the most treacherous thorns. Then you lift up Tiny Mailman very carefully, and bring him inside.

"Thank you," Tiny Mailman says.

"You are quite welcome," you say, like any normal seventh grader would.

Then you remember that Tiny Mailman had a tiny package! And it's a package for *you*!

"Can I open the tiny delivery now?" you ask.

"Yes," Tiny Mailman responds.

When you open the package, you find an amazing (tiny) piece of garlic bread. Chewing that buttery goodness reminds you of all that really matters in middle school and in life. And being reminded of that—and gleefully giddy that the space gnomes have not stolen *this* piece of garlic bread—*ha!*—you just have to laugh.

Yes: laugh.

Laugh! Laughing matters in middle school. Tiny mailmen and their problems matter, true, but laughing *really* matters.

When you find yourself caving or crumbling or hitting a wall, sometimes the best thing to do is watch a funny movie, or think of a funny joke, or listen for the doorbell, because, hey, it might be a Tiny Mailman out there waiting for you. Hurry, maybe you can help him (showing genuine kindness) before he gets stuck again!

THIRD ITEM OF STUFF: BE BRAVE

When I was in seventh grade, as you already know, I had no girl-friend, no basketball team to play for, and a thousand angry pimples screaming all over my face. Yet, I always noticed this girl walking through the halls. I'll call her Beenabeen. Beenabeen was a special education student, and she pretty much had her own classroom and worked with the special education teachers, so I wasn't around her that much, except for when I saw her in the hallways.

Well, one day, two guys who were much cooler and much more popular (and who each had a thousand less pimples than me) started teasing Beenabeen. They were acting stupid, making their voices sound low and strange, moving their arms around like they couldn't get them to function right. They were making fun of Beenabeen in that way that makes someone watching feel pissed off. And that's exactly how I felt: so angry that I wanted to kick their faces into the wall. Of course, kicking their faces into the wall would not have been a good choice. But doing *something* would have been a great choice. Going up to those guys and telling them to stop would have been a great choice. Going over and taking Beenabeen's hand and leading her away from those guys would have been a great choice. Going to get a teacher would have been a great choice.

Any of those possibilities would have been great because they would have been brave, and they would have been right.

Instead, I watched—angry at the guys for doing it and angry at myself for not doing something—until a teacher finally came along and broke it up.

Go to where the silence is and say something.

—Amy Goodman, contemporary journalist, investigative reporter, and columnist

The crazy thing about all of this is that I think about Beenabeen a lot. I can still see her in that hallway, and I can still see the boys taunting her. It was *decades* ago that I was where you are now—in middle school—but this thing with Beenabeen was like yesterday. And not a day goes by that I don't regret what I didn't do—the action I never took.

Sure, there's a lot about middle school I wish I could change. My pimples, for one. My fear of speaking in class, for another. My confusion and comparing myself to everyone else and so many other things. But if I could do middle school all over again and only had the chance to change one thing, it would be speaking up for Beenabeen.

That's it. That's the single thing I would really, *really* want to do differently. Maybe that's part of why I became a middle school teacher.

> True heroism is remarkably sober,
> very undramatic. It is not the urge to surpass
> all others at whatever cost, but the urge to serve
> others at whatever cost.
> —Arthur Ashe, international Tennis Hall of Fame inductee
> and activist

When it comes to being brave, you don't have to do anything huge or life changing. It takes one clear thing, really: speaking up when you know something isn't right. And the more you can think about the other stuff in middle school that matters, the more you'll notice people like Beenabeen. The more icebergs you notice, the more questions you'll ask, the more you wonder, the more connections you'll make—well, all of this is going to help you hold on to some amazing garlic bread, and it will help you share that amazing garlic bread with other people too!

Who is the Beenabeen in your school? Who is the Beenabeen in your life? Use your voice to support her, and you'll remember it (in a good way) forever. I promise.

FOURTH ITEM OF STUFF: ORGANIZE!

Ah, I know, I know. You read the word organize, and it's like somebody just told you that you have to eat buffalo eyeballs.

Organize.

Why are so many middle schoolers so scared of this word? Maybe it's because you hear organize and think, *Holy crap! That means a bunch of stuff that adults want me to do that I really have no clue how to do, but they're going to explain to me how to do it with lots of big words, and they'll hold up fancy-colored tabs and folders and sheets and binders, and I'll be thinking about my iPod, and when they're done talking, I WON'T EVEN KNOW WHAT THEY SAID!*

I hear you. I know how that feels. When I was in middle school, I shoved papers into any spot they could be shoved (including the garbage). I had no system for organizing.

So how do you *actually* organize yourself? Here are three things you can do today to help:

1. *Ignore the space gnomes shouting at you that you need to be able to do it all alone!* If you realize that your locker, binders, and life feel disorganized, then don't try to fix it all alone. Ask for help! This is something the space gnomes really don't want you to do. They want you to think that you need to be able to do it alone—which makes it easier for them

to steal all your garlic bread—but asking for help is also a brave thing. Think of a teacher, a parent, or even a friend who seems pretty kind and ask if they can help you go through your stuff and organize it.

2. *Every Friday, do a big dump!* Now, I don't mean a dump that you do in the bathroom. I mean, every Friday, stand by the recycling bin (in your homeroom or in your home) and do a quick flip through all your binders and backpack. Recycle all the papers that you're done with. Bam! Done! Recycled! This will help keep your backpack and binder (and even your life) a little bit less overwhelming.

3. *Talk!* Sometimes, if you feel disorganized, it might mean that you need to talk more about all the things in your heart and in your head. *Share what you're thinking and feeling.* Talk with your friends, talk with your teachers (seriously, we like it when students share with us—it's true!), talk with your parents, talk with your sisters and brothers . . . talk! Even just writing some of these thoughts in your journal can help. Share what you're thinking and feeling, and sometimes this helps your life feel a little less chaotic and disorganized. It might feel weird at first to talk about how you feel, but the more you do it the more normal it becomes. Soon, talking about feelings will be just as exciting as wolfing down a loaf of garlic bread!

FIFTH ITEM OF STUFF: WORK HARD EVEN WHEN YOU DON'T FEEL LIKE IT

You're thinking: *Man, this Luke Reynolds guy was a lot more fun when he was talking about love, and my parents being middle school students, and garlic bread. Why all this talk about organization and work now? Come on, man, can we talk about garlic bread some more?*

Soon. After all, there's always more to be said about the miracle of garlic bread. But remember, I promised to help you make your life meaningful in middle school, and to do so, this Fifth Item of Stuff is a big one. You've got to practice working hard even when you don't feel like it—*especially* when you don't feel like it, actually.

Notice that I used the word *practice* above. Working hard when you don't feel like it is never going to come easy, and you won't be able to do it well on your first, second, third, or fourth (or maybe even sixty-seventh) try. Why? *Because you don't feel like it.* If you decide to do only those things you feel like doing as a middle school student, you aren't going to do very much.

One of my students, Harold Haroldian, absolutely *did not* want to do the homework for English class. At night, students often have to read parts of a novel and write about them. Harold Haroldian never wanted to read or write at night. He would rather have a fight. Or get a shark bite, which may sound trite, but it's exactly right.

Where were we? Yes: Harold Haroldian never wanted to read and write for homework. And for three-quarters of the year, he didn't. And then, one day, he stayed after school and did the reading in the classroom. He looked up and said, "That was actually pretty interesting." Coming from Harold Haroldian, a line like that was about as awesome a line as I could imagine him saying!

One of my mentors once told me that "involvement precedes interest." What she meant was, sometimes, we have to do the work *before* we feel entirely interested or inspired by something. Like Harold Haroldian, sometimes we actually have to read and write (or do anything that you don't feel like doing at first) before it becomes interesting. Then, the more we work and the harder we work, the more interesting it becomes.

Now, we might not become enthralled. Taking out the garbage, for instance, is hard work, and our involvement with taking out the garbage might not make us hugely interested in, well, the garbage. However, it's hard work that matters! It's meaningful! It's kind and helps others. So sometimes the hard work helps get us interested, and sometimes the hard work is just a kind, helpful thing to do. Either way, you'll be better on the inside for doing the hard work on the outside.

SIXTH ITEM OF STUFF: BE KIND

Say hello to people in the hallways.

If someone drops something, pick it up.

If someone is crying, tell him or her that it will get better.

When someone lets you borrow a pencil, say, "Thank you, home slice." Or just "Thank you" will do fine, too, other people have assured me. (Although I prefer my method.)

If you see someone fall, don't laugh. Help that person up. Say, "I fall too."

Hold the door open for the person behind you.

Encourage your friends.

Help tiny mailmen who get stuck in flowerpots when they're delivering tiny packages.

Put some tasty garlic bread in the oven for your friends to enjoy.

Ask people questions. Really listen to their answers. Really listen to people's questions. Really give them thoughtful answers.

Exhaust the little moment. Soon it dies.
—Gwendolyn Brooks, a poet who was a master at using words to crack walls

Give a little money to someone in need. Even if you only get, say, an allowance of one buck a week, try giving away twenty cents of it. Or ten cents of it. Or five cents of it. You could drop it into a collection box at the checkout aisle of the grocery store. You could donate it online to an organization like Free the Slaves. (Check it out at freetheslaves.net. This group is trying to abolish slavery. Thought slavery was over and done with? Nope. There are still at least 21 million slaves in the world today. *Right now.* Check out the website.) You can always find a place to give your cents. The more you do this, the more you'll feel like you're really not alone in the world. I promise.

Notice people that no one else notices. Say hi to people most everyone ignores—people like janitors at your school, people at the checkout aisles in grocery stores, or really, really, super old people (the wrinkly kind).

Invite someone who sits alone to sit at your lunch table.

Say a few words each day to someone in your school who a lot of people either ignore or tease. Those few words will mean the world to this person.

SEVENTH ITEM OF STUFF: GO OUTSIDE

Wherever you live, chances are that you spend a lot of time indoors. Or that your friends spend a lot of time indoors. If you want to make your life meaningful in middle school, you've got to get away from advertisements and from the messages that bombard you when you're *inside*—whether in your home, at the mall, at your friend's house, or anywhere else with a roof up above.

When you get outside, under the open sky, or with the grass, pavement, or a stream beneath your feet, something seriously magical happens. You kind of separate yourself from the thousand voices telling you how to think, and this is what you hear instead—just a few voices that lead you to your own voice:

Sky: Hey! Welcome. I am huge, right? I mean, I am huge! Get lost in me for a bit. Hey, wait, wait—check this out: see my clouds?! Look how many there are! There are, like, hundreds of different shapes! What do you see? How do you feel?

Grass: Ah, hello, my noble friend! So glad to have you walk upon me! I know, not many people would utter such sentiments. But, ah, I am overjoyed by your presence. See my fullness, feel my slippery green blades brush your feet! Yes! The brightness of my soft blades! How do you feel? What do you think?

Pavement: Welcome, young friend. Dribble a basketball on me, ride a skateboard, kick a soccer ball, skip a rope, or draw with some chalk—hey, you're not **that** old that you can't draw with a little chalk when no one's looking. Or just walk all over me. When you move, what moves through you?

Stream: Sorry I can't talk long . . . rushing this way . . . just . . . enjoy!

The point is, when you get outside literally, you also kind of get outside figuratively. All that means is that you send your brain a signal when you go outside—and the message your brain gets is: *Ah, space! I can stretch out a bit, think for myself, and relax!*

In wildness is the preservation of the world.
—Henry David Thoreau, abolitionist, writer,
nature-lover who lived alone for two years

When you go outside and get away from shopping and posters and billboards, you cut way down on the overload your brain is used to from all the television, video games, smart phones (yep, maybe once in a while leave your phone inside while you go outside), and from so many other voices. This gives your brain a chance to kick back a little and get some distance from what it usually faces.

EIGHTH ITEM OF STUFF: SLEEP

You've got to sleep.

Got.

To.

Do.

It.

Why did I write that line that way—so grammatically incorrect and kind of annoying? Because:

I.

Really.

Want.

You.

To.

Get.

IT!

Okay, sorry, that was the last time. The truth is, your brain and body are built on sleep. Your whole human-being-system-thingy (*you*) is really like some amazingly magical robotic machine. You know the kind, right? In the movies, these robot machines of the future need special fuel or key codes or formulas to work properly and save the universe or the family or the kid.

Well, in real life, your body and brain are that super-cool robotic machine. Only they're not robotic. And they're not machines. But they do need a formula to run, and that formula is sleep. Sleep is incredibly important. I know you're going to want to stay up late texting friends under the covers at night when you should be sleeping (don't get any ideas if you don't already do this). But if you miss out on sleep, you are kind of deep frying your brain. You are going to feel like every little thing that goes wrong is a *huge deal and signifies the end of the world as you know it.*

But it doesn't.

You.

Just.

Need.

To.

Get.

More.

Sleep.

(I'm sorry, I seriously couldn't resist. But I swear that's the last time in this entire book you'll ever see me do this. Hey, you're almost finished anyway, right?)

NINTH ITEM OF STUFF: HUG YOUR PARENTS

You're going to feel, sometimes, like you don't have a clue who you are, and that the whole world is against you, and that nothing about you is right, and that nothing is going your way (nor will anything *ever* go your way). This feeling comes to everyone in middle school—and in life, for that matter. But, like we talked about earlier, the feeling will pass. It will head for the hills.

(By the way, what's that burning smell? Is that garlic bread you put in the oven for you and your friends back during the Sixth Item of Stuff still in there? It is? Quick, go get it out, quick! There are few things more tragic than a burned loaf of garlic bread.)

So the feeling will pass. But in the meantime, while you're having that feeling, your parents are going to be really, really confused. They are sometimes going to feel like they don't know how to talk to you. They are going to feel like you changed into this entirely different person, *overnight*! Your parents are going to feel confused and worried and maybe a little scared for you.

Hug them every once in a while. You don't have to do it all the time or have any particular reason at all. You don't even have to say anything. Just give them a hug. I promise that it will help them, and it will even help *you* make your life more meaningful in middle school. This hugging of your parents not only will feel good (hey, come on, admit it:

hugs feel pretty darn awesome, even from your parents), but it will also help your parents feel more connected to you. And remember: Connections rock! Connections are freaking awesome!

TENTH ITEM OF STUFF: WRITE

Ah, but this guy's an English teacher! OF COURSE he's going to tell me to write!

Okay, fine, I'll give you that point. But I'm not talking about writing amazing stories or penning a bunch of remarkable poems (though, if you want to do that, awesome!).

What I *am* talking about is journaling. Whether you're feeling good or bad—whether you're happy and glowing like the sun or you're feeling like a pile of stinking crap (and I'm talking about *a big pile of stinky crap*)—just write down a few thoughts, emotions, ideas, worries, or hopes.

Wait a minute, there, Luke—wait just one minute—if you're telling me to write when I feel good or bad, then you're telling me to write all the time. Aren't you?

You got it. But you don't have to write a lot. Even a few sentences will help. What this act of writing does is it lets some steam out of your brain. (And the other thing writing does, by the way, is that it infuriates the space gnomes. As soon as they see you writing, they go crazy, because writing makes you grow stronger in a whole load of ways, and when you grow stronger, it won't be nearly as easy to steal your garlic bread.)

When things are either good or bad, your brain is working hard to make sense of it all. If you don't write a little about it, you're forcing your brain to do all the work, all the time. When you write it down, you can take a little bit of the weight off your brain and put it on the paper. Paper is fine with this—I know. I checked, and it told me the exact following words: "Of course I'm fine with students putting some of their feelings and thoughts down on me. Hey, what else would I be doing? I'll tell you what: I'd be sitting here, doing absolutely nothing, completely bored *out of my mind.*"

So if you write down some of your emotions and experiences and thoughts, not only will you be taking a load off your brain, you'll also be helping Paper feel more useful. (Plus, after middle school, you can look back at all of what you wrote and smile, or laugh, or cry, or say, "Hmmm," in that really deep kind of thinking way.)

These ten Items of Stuff can help you enormously to create meaningful moments and incredible possibilities in middle school. But the even cooler thing about these ten Items of Stuff is that they can help do the same thing for the people *around* you. When you show kindness, or when you laugh, or when you work hard, or make wise decisions for your body, like sleeping well, all of this helps you grow and become more yourself. But it also helps others do the same for themselves. You start changing the way you interact with other people, and they see a new kind of light in your life. (Not some kind of eerie, creepy light, like a greenish glow that emerges from behind your head while your eyes start glowing red, and then spooky music starts playing in the background. If this happens, look around for space gnomes—they might be trying to invade!)

This new kind of light in your life is more like the glow of the moon at night. Or the stars poking through the blanket of dark that covers the Earth each time the sun goes down. All of us—all those middle school students you walk past each day, and even those teachers in whose classrooms you sit, and even your parents (who may be overgrown middle school students)—notice when other people bring a little extra light into this world. And by following these ten Items of Stuff, you make yourself lighter, and you become a light for others. I've seen it happen, and the effect is, well, beautiful. It's something the space gnomes can never, ever steal.

CONCLUSION

A nd that's it. Ten chapters full of garlic, secrets, and space gnomes. As you go through middle school (and through high school, and college, and life), keep going back and rereading parts of this book. After all, you don't want to one day become a vastly overgrown middle school student, do you?

Whatever happens during middle school, I promise you that you can make your life meaningful during the journey. I believe in you.

I know, I know. You're probably thinking, *How can you believe in me if you haven't even met me?!* Well, truthfully, you haven't really taken much initiative to try to meet me, have you? I mean, have you even emailed me yet? My wife and I (and our sons) would be delighted to meet you, and if you live close by or happen to be in town visiting, we'll have you and your parents over for a nice Italian meal—with more loaves of garlic bread than you could ever dream about. And if you and your parents *do* end up coming over for all these amazing loaves of garlic bread, we'll talk together about how we defeated the space gnomes each time they tried to rob us, or lie to us, or make us think that surfaces are all that matters!

Until that day, you'll have to trust me when I say that *I do believe in you.* I've taught students just like you, and I believed in every single one of them. And I was once a student just like you, and somewhere along the way I learned to believe in myself.

You'll learn to believe in yourself too. You can start practicing now by doing some of the things you learned right here.

You began this book by reading about my very first day of middle school, which (once I was finally honest) you got to see was pretty bad. And I wish that right now, in this conclusion, I could tell you that my *last* day of middle school was the exact opposite. I wish I could tell you that I learned all of this stuff, and I put it into practice, and I defeated the space gnomes, and I ate gobs and gobs (and gobs!) of garlic bread.

But that would be a lie.

My last day of middle school was actually pretty similar to my first day of middle school. I had learned a few things, sure, but I still felt incredibly awkward and out of place and afraid, and not knowing anything about icebergs and caked dirt and garlic bread and so many other things that *you now know.*

But the true thing (and the cool thing) is this: I get to see a different journey with many students every day. I get to see their eyes, and their actions, and their words, and their decisions as they learn about icebergs and garlic bread, about caked dirt and grades. And their last days of middle school are different from their first days. Not perfect—no, not by a long shot—but better. They try to put some of this stuff into practice, and I see life becoming different, lighter, better. They learn to fend off the space gnomes and retain their amazing garlic bread. And that's the whole deal—that's surviving middle school.

**It is not in the still calm of life . . .
that great characters are formed. . . .
Great necessities call out great virtues.**
—Abigail Adams, American colonial-era woman of great boldness
and political brilliance

So how about it? Why not go give your parents a hug right now? Or see what it feels like to be caked dirt? Or ask your teacher a bunch of interesting questions? Or count to ten before you make your next decision? Or tell that voice of comparison to *shut up*? Or stop trying to look like a poster you saw in the mall? Or practice knowing that you are totally complete *on your* own, without a girlfriend or boyfriend? Or do that homework even though you don't feel like it? Or laugh? Just laugh—right now—go for it. Make it a big belly laugh, the kind that starts in your gut and lunges from your mouth like a fugitive on the run (not that tiny fugitives have ever hidden in your mouth or anything like that).

Go ahead. Why not try it? What have you got to lose? You can keep on doing it the way everyone else does, or you can try something a little bit different . . . something a little more . . . well, a little more *you*. And what the world desperately needs right now is exactly that.

It needs you.

ACKNOWLEDGMENTS

Growing up, I had a number of teachers who cared deeply about me. These teachers showed great passion for their subjects and yet also love and concern for all their students. Foremost among this group is the incomparable Mr. Robert Looney. Thank you for your energy, your kindness, and your wisdom. And to my other teachers from Windsor, Connecticut, who made learning a journey of exploration and joy: Mr. Hooper, Mr. Norton, Mrs. Ferrero, Mr. Scheer, Mrs. Beauregard, Mrs. Malnotti, Mrs. Giardi, Ms. George, Mr. Whalen, Mr. Grant, and Mr. Shea—thank you each for your love of learning and of students.

To my agent, Ammi-Joan Paquette! Thank you for hearing the idea for this goofy, strange, crazy, zany (adjectives ensue!) project and believing in it from the get-go. Thanks for sharing in the hope that its message and style would reach and inspire students. And, what's more, thanks for believing in the power of words and the power of people to connect and try to make the world just a little bit better and a little more fun. I could never have predicted the incredible journey. I am deeply grateful to you for every step of the way.

To my editor at Beyond Words: Nicole Geiger. Yes! Thank you for your incredible support of the project, your insightful eye, and your belief in the message that drives this book. Your love of creativity and authenticity made the work and revisions enormously fun, and I am so grateful for your ideas, questions, comments, and hopes for this book. From the beginning, your energy on behalf of this project was inspiring, and I love how you shepherded it from stage to stage with infectious enthusiasm and unflagging commitment. Thank you so much! You have been a joy to work with.

To my developmental editor, Ali McCart: thank you! You brought positivity, an uncanny eye for seeing how the parts work together to make the whole, and a zest and zeal for the project that inspired and invigorated me. In our rounds of back-and-forth editing, you helped to find key spots to change and revise and expand and condense, and the result is a much stronger book than we ever would have had without your keen eye, big heart, and wise counsel. Thank you for your work ethic, energy, and expertise!

Thank you to everyone at Beyond Words: Henry Covey, my copyeditor who provided insightful analysis, revisions, and excellent modifications that strengthened both the voice and the meaning of this book; Lindsay Easterbrooks-Brown, my managing editor, who oversaw every phase of this book's journey, round after round, and was dedicated to encouraging its often weird premise and examples; production editor Emmalisa Sparrow, who also provided copyediting help and wisdom. And to Leah Brown and Sara Blum, beautiful work! Thank you all for your energy and excitement and work!

To my brothers Chris, Mike, Bryan, and Matt: you guys are the best friends in the world, and I love how you debunk the status quo at every turn, choosing instead to be authentic and honest. I love laughing with you, learning with you, and seeing the world in new ways every time we're together. And to my parents, Harry and Kathy Reynolds, thank you for modeling what it means to constantly revise—both in work and in life. You show me that love is all about fighting to grow and learn and see other people and situations in new ways.

To Paul and Diana Gant, Susan and Wendell Anderson, David Anderson, Harold Fenton, sister-in-law Mandy, cousins Caleb and Evan Reynolds, Wade Austin, Phil and Kate Anderson, Matt Bednarz, Brian Daniels, Russ Crist, Mike Dunn, Chris Doyle, Jamahl Hines, Mike Baxer, Patti Guignino, Deb Jeffers, Jim Carter, Audrey Mika, Ann Cummins, John Dufresne, Kathy Erskine, Tamara Ellis Smith, Mike Jung, Paul Borgman, Brian Blake, Spencer Zeigler, Peggy Quill, Laurie Curley, Davida Bagatelle, Mary Jane Shelton, Jane Thompsen, Janis Dyer, Wyatt Holt, Mike Dessarro, and Rich and Joan Fenton, who all are supportive, kind, lovely people who care about kids, about stories, and about the power of people to change the world. Thank you each for your examples and your many kindnesses.

To my own students—from those I began with in Farmington, Connecticut, to Flagstaff, Arizona, to Hudson, Massachusetts, to York, England, and finally to Harvard, Massachusetts. You have each taught me so very much about life, and you've shown me the meaning of courage, change, and possibility. I thank you each for your incredible efforts, your brave journeys, and your kind hearts. *You* are both the reason and the inspiration for this book, and in no uncertain terms: this book is yours. Especially to Adriel Gomez: thank you for your beautiful life and the way you fought for hope and love. We all miss you.

And finally, to my own family: Tyler and Benjamin, while there is so much I want to teach you about the world, I know that you'll end up teaching me much more than I ever could teach you. Already, you've shown me much about making mistakes and moving on, finding joy in hard places, learning to laugh at ourselves, cool dance moves, various kinds of squelching noises, and love. Especially about love. And Jennifer, walking hand in hand through many crazy adventures, you make the meaning and message of this book not only real for me, but you also form it and re-form it every day that you live. You teach me how to take risks, overcome fear, and especially how to see the larger story at work in our lives and in the world around us. Thank you for your love, and thank you for your desire to live differently and boldly. Every word of this book would not exist were it not for your support, hope, kindness, belief, and love. Always the love. Thank you, my pilgrim soul.

RECOMMENDED RESOURCES

Throughout this book, you've read some stories and embraced some new ideas and found some quotes from pretty neat people. And you've learned a heck of a lot about space gnomes, garlic bread, and making your journey through middle school meaningful.

But your mission through middle school can be inspired in some other pretty awesome and fun ways too. Here's a list of some very cool books, websites, and movies that you might check out to help you along your journey. (Of course, such a list would not be complete without me poking my nosey nose in to share a few things about each, right?)

BOOKS

The Absolute Value of Mike by Kathryn Erskine (Philomel Books, 2011)
This novel is an incredibly funny book that shows us that one kind of success (grades or achievement, for example) is *not* what life is all about.

Be a Changemaker: How to Start Something That Matters by Laurie Ann Thompson (Beyond Words/Simon Pulse, 2014)
This nonfiction book explores all the ways you can make a difference in the world, with great true stories and examples of other students doing just that.

The Breadwinner by Deborah Ellis (Groundwood Books, 2001)
This stunning novel shares the story of a girl named Parvana, who lives in Afghanistan and fights against the unjust Taliban rule in her own small way. This book shows us what it means to be heroic in any way we can—and to believe that things can get better.

Eighth-Grade Superzero by Olugbemisola Rhuday-Perkovich (Arthur A. Levine Books, 2011)
This incredible novel shows us Reggie, a character who's nicknamed "Pukey" and is judged and rejected by students at his school. However, as he gets involved with a local homeless shelter, his life changes, and he begins to see what truly matters in life.

Geeks, Girls, and Secret Identities by Mike Jung (Arthur A. Levine Books, 2012)
This novel disrupts all kinds of stereotypes through a cast of memorable, vivid, and incredibly fun (and funny) characters and plotlines. It goes way beneath the top 10 percent of an iceberg, and it's a super-fun read!

Okay for Now by Gary D. Schmidt (Clarion Books, 2011)
This novel shows us that kindness and courage trump all kinds of pain and meanness in the world. Doug is a character you will love, who will inspire you to find out what parts of you are hiding deep inside.

The Skin I'm In by Sharon G. Flake (Hyperion, 2007)

This is a beautiful novel about a girl named Maleeka Madison who is a poet battling her way through middle school. While others in her school taunt Maleeka for the dark color of her skin, Maleeka learns to see her own beauty, her own power, and to embrace the strength of her own voice.

WEBSITES

The Learning Network (nytimes.com/learning)

This website is hosted by the *New York Times* and includes awesome ways to learn about what's happening in the world. There are great videos, interesting articles, cool words to learn, and connections between what's happening in your life and what's happening all around the world.

Peace Corps Kids World (peacecorps.gov/kids)

This website offers some incredible information on projects and activities all around the world through playing the Peace Corps Challenge game. You can learn about challenges, service projects, and ways to make a difference.

Teen Ink (teenink.com)

This is a fabulous website where you can read all kinds of student writing and work, including poetry, nonfiction, short stories, and interviews. You'll see that you're not alone in your hopes, fears, and experiences—and you'll also get a chance to see some of the 90 percent of the iceberg from other students' lives. Plus, you can even submit your own creative work to this magazine—as many of my students have!

MOVIES & DOCUMENTARIES

Apollo 13 (Universal Pictures, 1995)
This movie is the incredible true story of the three astronauts who were supposed to land on the moon. However, their ship encountered problems, and their mission changed to just staying alive and returning safely to Earth. Instead of getting the A+ for making it to the moon, many might have seen their mission as a failure—and yet the film shows us that something deeper than a grade was at work on this mission.

Emmanuel's Gift (Lookalike Productions, 2007)
This is a remarkable documentary that is based on the true story of Emmanuel Ofosu Yeboah, a man who was born with only one working leg. In Ghana, where he was born, the culture had told him he was worthless because of this physical deformity. But instead of listening to that message, Emmanuel learned how to ride a bike with one leg, and he rode clear across his entire country.

Glory Road (Buena Vista Pictures, 2006)
This is the incredible story of the 1965–66 Texas Western Miners men's basketball team and their march to the NCAA Championship. In their final game, only the black players on the team played on the court, as a powerful message against the racism that was rampant in college and professional sports during this time period.

Killing Us Softly 4: Advertising's Image of Women (Cambridge Documentary Films, 2010)
Jean Kilbourne hosts this important documentary that explores how advertising can often trick girls and women into thinking that certain ways of dressing, behaving, thinking, and relating are essential.

However, what really matters is being authentically *you*—not who advertisers tell you to be.

A Place at the Table (Magnolia Pictures, 2013)
This moving documentary explores hunger and poverty in America, and it offers up ways we can learn to help. It will show you different stories as well as explore overarching structures that allow poverty and hunger to continue. But it will also give you hope to make a difference.

Rudy (TriStar Pictures, 1993)
This is one of my all-time favorite movies. In my classroom, there's a massive poster of this movie. It's the true story of Daniel "Rudy" Ruettiger, who is a small kid who dreams of playing football for the University of Notre Dame. While everyone tells him there's no way this is ever going to be possible, Rudy doesn't listen. (Talk about caked dirt!)

Tough Guise: Violence, Media, and the Crisis in Masculinity (Media Education Foundation, 1999)
This documentary powerfully explores how boys receive messages of violent toughness through movies and music. However, instead of believing the lie that "real men are tough," the documentary shows us that boys and men can be sensitive, kind, and gentle. Courage is not violence.

NOTES

CHAPTER 2

1. George Plimpton, "Ernest Hemingway, The Art of Fiction No. 21," *The Paris Review*, no. 18 (Spring 1958), http://www.theparisreview.org/interviews/4825/the-art-of-fiction-no-21-ernest-hemingway.

CHAPTER 3

2. Kathiann M. Kowalski, "Rewiring the Brain," *Odyssey* 10, no. 3 (2001): 12.
3. Samuel G. Solomon and Adam Kohn, "Moving Sensory Adaptation beyond Suppressive Effects in Single Neurons," *Current Biology* 24, no. 20 (2014): R1012–R1022.

CHAPTER 4

4. Nick Haslam, *Psychology in the Bathroom* (Hampshire, UK: Palgrave Macmillan, 2012): 5.

CHAPTER 5

5. Lance Allred, *Enchanted Rock: A Natural and Human History* (Austin, TX: University of Texas Press, 2009): 77.
6. Henri Nouwen, *The Inner Voice of Love: A Journey Through Anguish to Freedom* (NY: Doubleday, 1996).

CHAPTER 6

7. Richard M. Ingersoll, "Beginning Teacher Induction: What the Data Tell Us," *Education Week* (May 16, 2012), http://www.edweek.org/ew/articles/2012/05/16/kappan_ingersoll.h31.html.

CHAPTER 8

8. Plato, *The Republic of Plato*, trans. Allan Bloom (NY: Basic Books, 1991): 193-97.

Made in the USA
Las Vegas, NV
15 March 2023